THE *Quiltmaker* COLLECTION

Quilting Motifs

VOLUME 2

*A collection of quilting patterns
from* QUILTMAKER's *first 20 years*

By the staff of QUILTMAKER
Edited by Maria Reardon Capp
Additional art work by Annie Segal

PRIMEDIA Consumer Media & Magazine Group
741 Corporate Circle, Ste. A
Golden, Colorado 80401-0101

Additional copies are available for purchase for U.S. $14.95.
Please call 1-800-590-3465 within USA. Outside USA,
phone 720-836-1123 or 800-590-3465.

Editor: Maria Reardon Capp
Quilting motif designs: *QUILTMAKER* staff
Additional artwork and book design: Annie Segal
Photography: Mellisa Karlin Mahoney

First Printing 2002
Manufactured in the United States of America
ISBN: 0-9713713-1-8

Table of Contents

Charm Tacks™

Motifs and Variations

Welcome

Welcome to Volume 2 of *The QUILTMAKER Collection: Quilting Motifs.* This volume features motifs from the garden—flowers, leaves, bugs and butterflies; motifs for children's quilts including a unicorn, dragon, and princess; and classic motifs of cables and feathers.

For many years, our magazine has been trusted for clear and accurate step-by-step directions for making a quilt—from start to finish. This includes beautiful quilting motifs to enhance your patchwork or applique, and more recently beautiful continuous-line quilting motifs for the ever-increasing number of machine quilters. This volume represents a variety of motif styles and sizes spanning *QUILTMAKER'S* 20 years in publication. Many variations on each motif provide ideas and alternatives for every project. And for those with specific requirements, we include an extensive index that allows you to search for a motif based either on a theme or the size of space requiring quilting.

We hope you find this collection an invaluable and inspiring resource as you select the perfect designs to create the rich surface textures of your quilt.

How to Use This Book

Please note that the measurements for the quilt blocks and borders are finished sizes into which the motifs can fit. Seam allowances are already hidden by the time you get to the quilting step.

To find a motif to fit a specific space, refer to the Size Index for suggestions.

See the Table of Contents if you have a themed quilt and want a motif as specific as animals, mystic, or even '60s motifs.

When you need quilting inspiration, just leaf through the pages.

Selecting Motifs

Answering these questions will help narrow down motif possibilities.

What is the style of my quilt?
For a formal, traditional quilt, look for circular motifs, feathers or flowers. You can enhance the formal style of your quilt by centering motifs on each plain block.

If you're working for an informal, casual look, less defined shapes work well. You may want to position motifs randomly or use a combination of motifs in different areas to enhance the style.

Do I want to enhance or contrast the lines of the quilt top?
If your quilt is made up of diagonals that you want to enhance, choose an angular, geometric motif. If you want to soften the appearance of the diagonal lines, choose a gentler and more rounded motif.

What size space do I need to fill?
Our size index will help you find a motif to fit your space. If the motif you choose doesn't have an option that fits, see "Adapting Motifs" on page 7.

Does the space I need to fill have a busy print or a plain print?
Solid colored fabric is the perfect place to showcase the intricate quilting motifs you love. The same motif on a busy print fabric will get lost, and all your quilting will go unnoticed.

Am I machine quilting or hand quilting?
Hand quilting allows most any kind of design without limitations. Make sure you find a motif that will showcase all the time you put into the quilting.

If machine quilting is your method of choice, you may want to start your search in the Subject Index with continuous-line patterns. You can complete individual motifs without having to start and stop sewing. If you select a motif that is not a continuous-line pattern, keep in mind that you will have to begin and end the line wherever it dead-ends. Make sure to start and stop these lines of quilting with tiny stitches to prevent them from pulling out.

How accomplished am I as a quilter?
If the thought of quilting even one of those detailed motifs strikes fear in your heart, choosing it for your queen-sized quilt project will only mean that the quilt never gets done. Choose something simpler that you will be happy with, saving the detailed motif for a pillow top that requires only one design. If you love to quilt and can't wait to tackle the biggies, go for it!

Adapting Motifs

You've found a motif you love, but for one reason or another it isn't exactly right. Here are some ways to work with the motif you can't live without.

Change the size

The easiest way to adjust the size of a motif is with a photocopy machine. First, make a paper shape that represents the patch for the motif. Then reduce or enlarge the motif on the copier until it fits into the paper shape. Layering the two papers and holding them up to a light is a good way to check.

Consider an alternative placement

Who says a motif has to fit inside a block? If your motif is too large, perhaps it can break the boundaries of the block and overlap into other areas of the quilt. If it fits the style of the quilt, why not?

If your motif is too small, consider multiples in the same block, or randomly place them over the surface of the quilt. This is especially effective with leaves, small flowers or stars that scatter randomly in nature just as they can on your quilt.

Consider filling in the space with other quilting

If your motif is small and you don't want multiple shapes but need more quilting, use another method such as those shown at right to fill in the space.

For a formal look, add a grid of quilting behind the motif.

Machine stipple all around the motif to cover areas quickly and make the motif stand out.

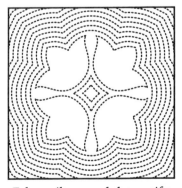

Echo quilt around the motif to emphasize the shape of the central motif.

Marking Your Quilts

Marking for hand quilting

- A light pencil line is often all you need. The line will be covered by the quilting thread, and little or no erasing is necessary.
- If you are quilting ¼″ from seam allowances, consider using tape as described in the **Marking Tools Table** on page 8.
- Most hand quilters mark quilt tops before basting.

Marking for machine quilting

- The line must be clearly visible to make the machine's path easy to follow.
- When you trace a motif, plan the path the machine will take. This will give you some practice before actually quilting.
- Tracing paper, contact paper and freezer paper are all great alternatives to marking your quilt. See the **Marking Tools Table** on page 8 for more information.

Making Templates

To make a template for a marking technique that requires tracing, you will need heavy clear plastic. Trace the motif on the plastic using a permanent marker. If the design is closed, simply cut on the marked outer line. For a more intricate motif, use an X-Acto® knife to cut out the lines, cutting a wide enough channel to accommodate your marking tool. You can also buy a double-bladed knife made specifically for cutting channels.

Marking Tools

Every quilter will have her favorite way of marking a quilt for one reason or another.
This table helps you identify tools to find your own preferences.

Product	Description	Type of Quilting	Advantages	Concerns	Requires a template?
Pencil	Quilter's colored pencils Mechanical pencils	Hand	Thin line usually disappears under stitching Easily erased	Often not dark enough to be seen for machine quilting	yes
Chalk	Tailor's chalk Chalk dispensers Chalk pencils	Hand/ Machine	Comes in a variety of colors Erases easily with rubbing	Can rub off before you want it to	yes
Soap	Soapstone Soap slivers	Hand	Easily washed out Economical Shows well on dark fabrics	Often not dark enough to be seen on light fabrics and prints	yes
Markers	Air-erase markers Washable markers	Hand/ Machine	Good dark line	Some quilters worry about marks reappearing	yes
Hera marker	Tool that "creases" the quilt to show markings	Hand/ Machine	Makes no permanent mark	Can be difficult to see Can wear off before you want it to	yes
Tape	Masking tape Narrow tape with marked lines	Hand/ Machine	Peels off easily Marking of the quilt top is not necessary Can be reused	Only for straight lines or very gentle curves	no
Quilter's guide on machine	Bar attaches to the walking foot on some machines	Machine	Marking of the quilt top is not necessary	Best for straight lines with a guide to follow	no
Tracing paper	Motif is traced on the paper and pinned to quilt top	Machine	Marking of the quilt top is not necessary	Motif must be traced on every sheet	no
Contact paper, Freezer paper	Motif is traced on paper and cut out, then stuck to quilt	Machine	Reuseable several times Marking of the quilt top is not necessary	For outline design only If stitches puncture paper, can be difficult to remove	no

Positioning Motifs and Using the Variations in This Book

Finding the Center

For a centered motif, find the center of the block or patch by folding the fabric in half lengthwise and then crosswise and lightly finger pressing. When unfolded, the creases will help you center the motif for tracing.

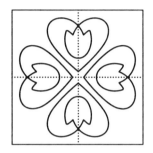

Finding Diagonal Lines

Many variations are lined up with diagonal lines. To find these, cut a piece of tracing paper to the size of the finished block or patch. Fold in half from corner to corner and then fold in half again. When unfolded, the creases can be used to line up motifs to create the whole design.

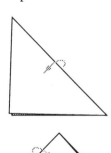

Finding Vertical, Horizontal and Diagonal Lines

To recreate some designs, you may need guide lines in several directions. Fold the paper lengthwise and crosswise, then open it out and refold it corner to corner to get horizontal, vertical and diagonal lines.

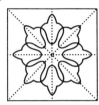

Eight-Point Circles

Some design options rely on circles for motif placement. You will find a ¼-circle template on page 94. The template includes all the circle sizes used in this book. To draw a circular motif, first find the center of your tracing paper by folding. Next, open up the paper, align the center marks and trace the arc. Then, rotating the paper ¼ turn each time, repeat the tracing to make a complete circle.

For example, a 12″ block for the Floral Spray motif on page 29 has eight flowers evenly spaced around an 10″ circle. To draw this design, place a dot where each fold crosses the circle. Line up the flower motif

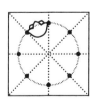

with the dots, trace, and repeat until the circle of flowers is complete.

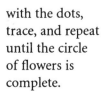

Six-Point Circles

A variation for the Winding Way motif on page 14 uses only six flowers. To draw this design, draw a 9½″ circle, and then use the angle template on page 94 to draw lines at 60° angles, as shown.

Place a dot where each line crosses the circle and line up the motif

between the dots. Trace the flower and rotate and repeat until the circle of flowers is complete.

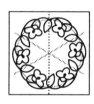

Another example of a six-point circle is a variation of the Jaunty Jump-Ups motif on page 48. Draw a 4½″ circle and mark lines at 60° angles as shown. Place three dots on the circle, one at every other intersection of the lines and the circle.

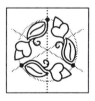

Starting at each dot, trace the partial motif three times. In this case, the circle becomes part of the quilting design. Be sure to trace it when transferring the design to the quilt top.

And now on to the designs!

Evening Trumpet

Reversed motifs
are shown in gray.

4½"

15"

Evening Trumpet

4½"

Reversed motifs are shown in gray.

4½"

8"

5½"

6"

10"

8½"

11"

9½"

Celestial

3½"

3½"

5"

8"

6"

6"

8"

Lilac Leaf

Reversed motifs
are shown in gray.

3"

2½"

9"

6"

8½"

9"

8"

6½"

10½"

13"

Winding Way

Start

Arrows indicate direction for continuous-line machine quilting.

3½"

3½"

Reversed motifs are shown in gray.

3"

3"

10"

8"

8½"

8"

11½"
(9½" circle)

12"
(9½" circle)

Granny Smith's

3"

2½"

7½"

5"

7½"

12"

6½"

**Butterfly
Charm Tack**

Celtic Chain

4½"

5"

5"

7"

8"

Celebration

3"

3"

Reversed motifs are shown in gray.

4"

6½"

9½"

7½"

13"

9½"

9½"

Daisy Field

5½"

7"

10"

10"

7"

Daisy Field

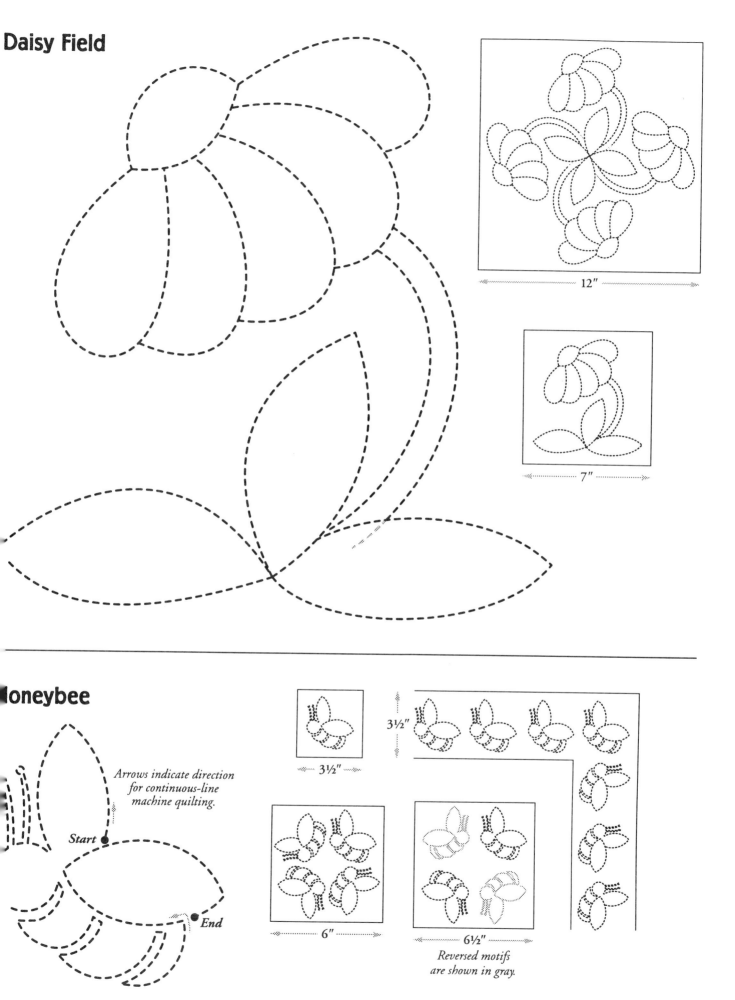

12"

7"

Honeybee

Arrows indicate direction for continuous-line machine quilting.

Start

End

3½"

3½"

6"

6½"

Reversed motifs are shown in gray.

Fluttering Leaves

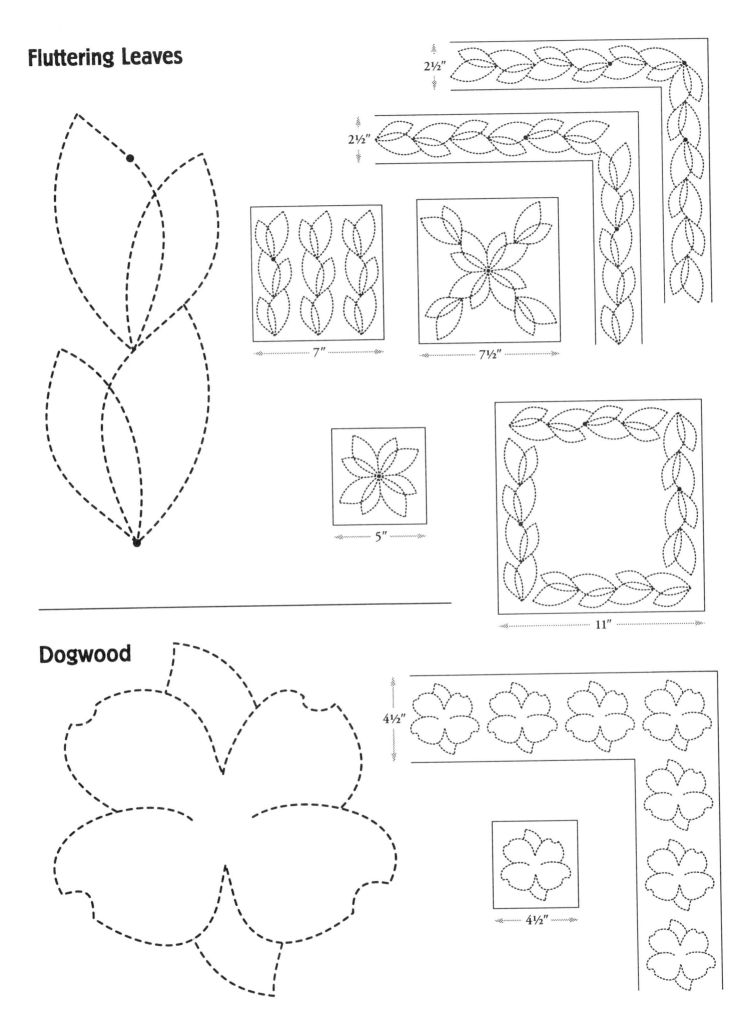

2½"

2½"

7"

7½"

5"

11"

Dogwood

4½"

4½"

Bamboo

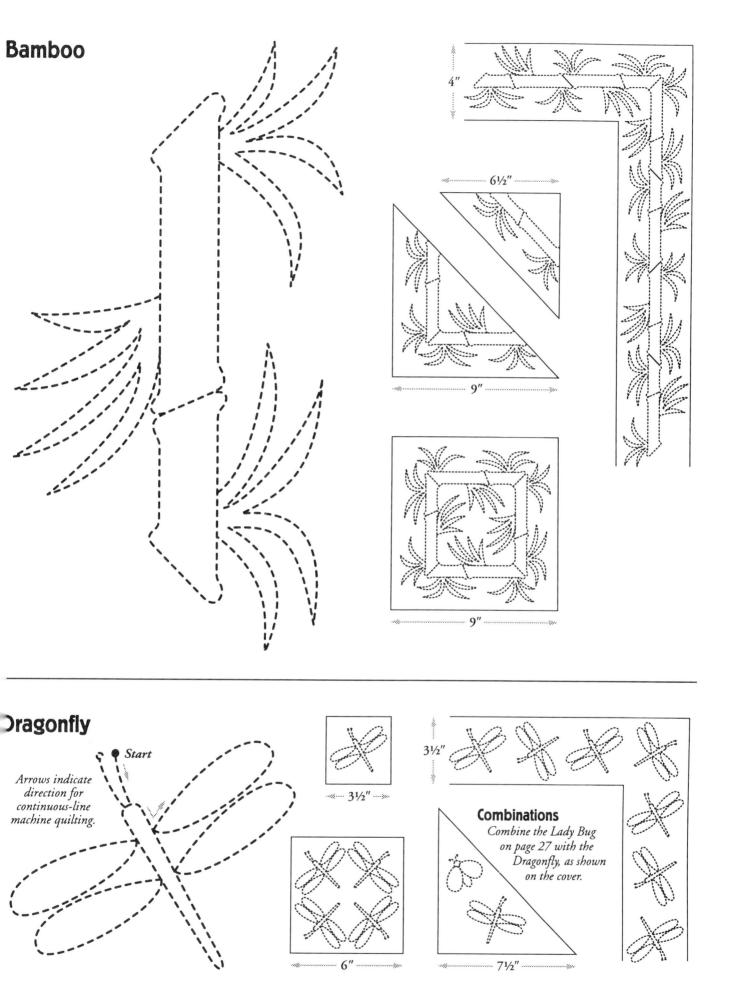

Dragonfly

● **Start**

Arrows indicate direction for continuous-line machine quilting.

3½"

3½"

Combinations

Combine the Lady Bug on page 27 with the Dragonfly, as shown on the cover.

6"

7½"

Springtime

Rondo

Reversed motifs are shown in gray.

6"

4"

5½"

7½"

7

10"

13"

Feather Wreath

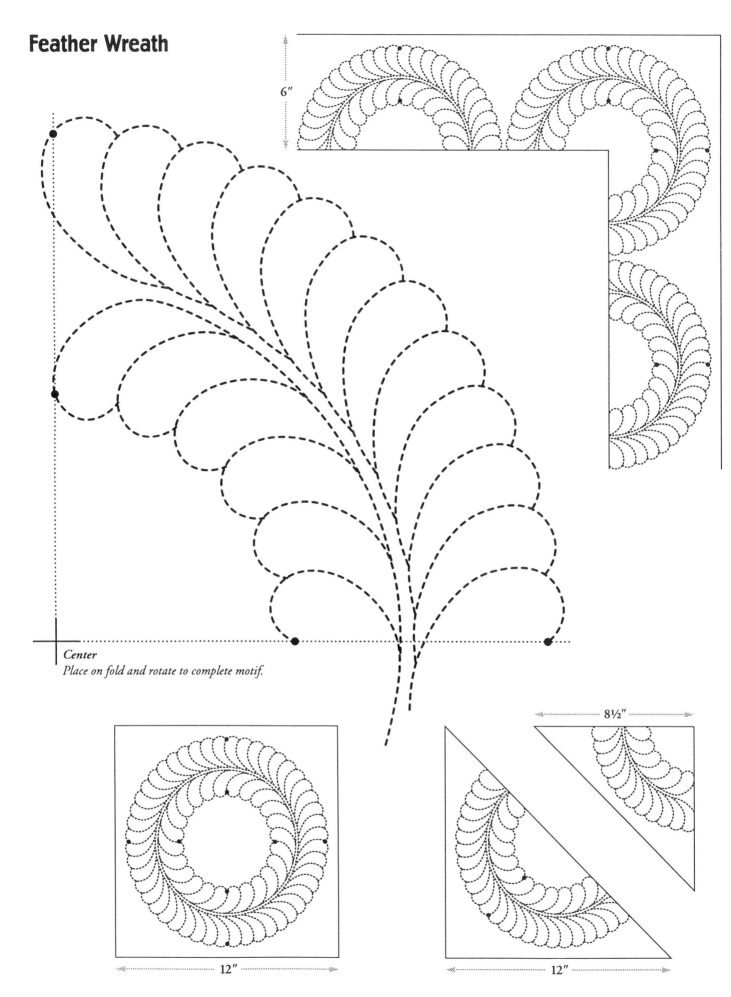

Center
Place on fold and rotate to complete motif.

6″

8½″

12″

12″

Berry Blossom

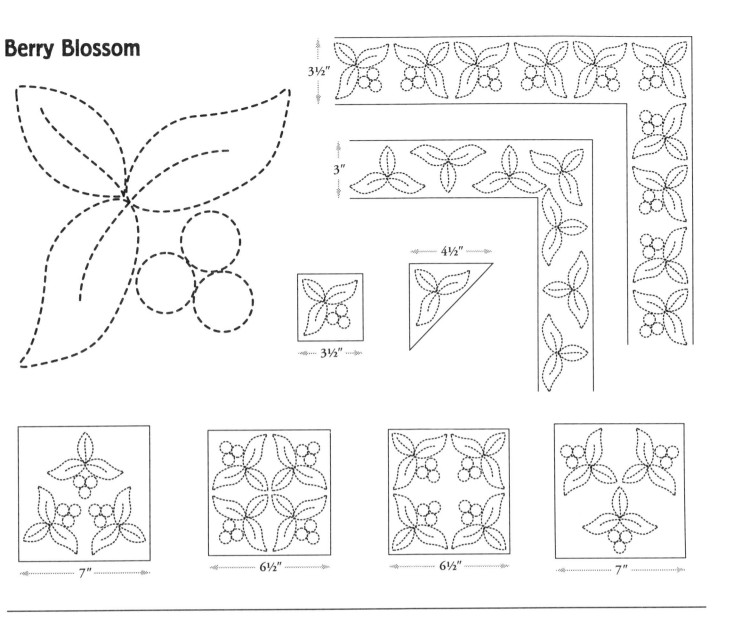

Graceful Vine

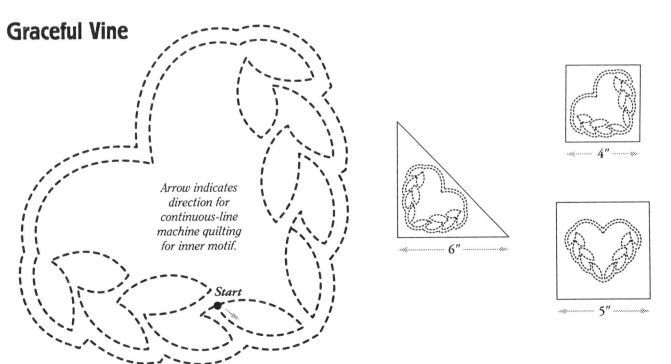

Arrow indicates direction for continuous-line machine quilting for inner motif.

Start

Autumn Leaves

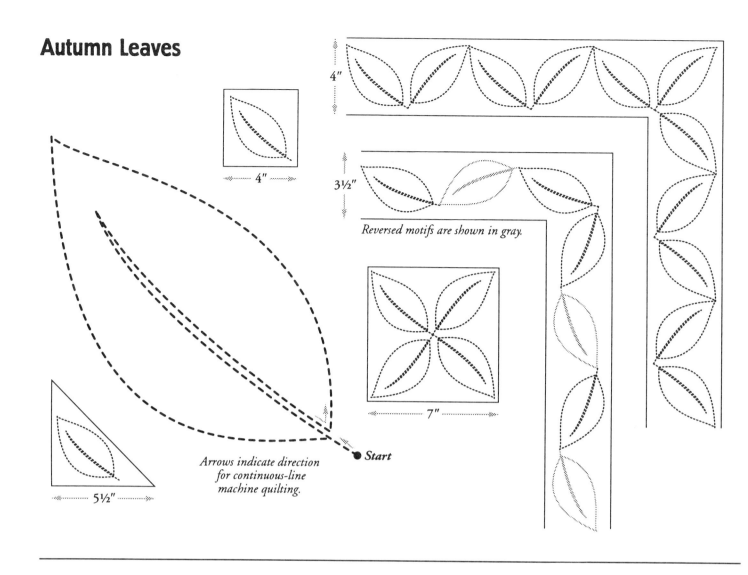

4"

4"

3½"

Reversed motifs are shown in gray.

7"

5½"

Arrows indicate direction for continuous-line machine quilting.

● **Start**

Barn Swallow

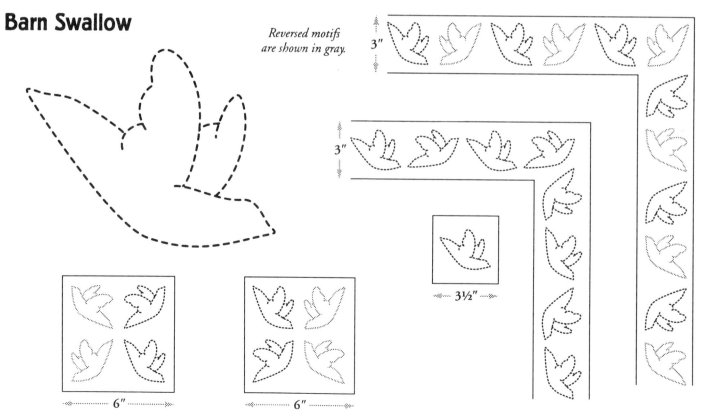

Reversed motifs are shown in gray.

3"

3"

3½"

6"

6"

Lady Bug

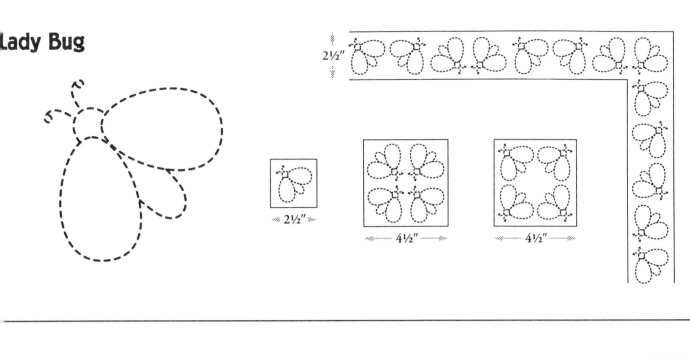

2½"

2½"

4½"

4½"

Fortune Flower

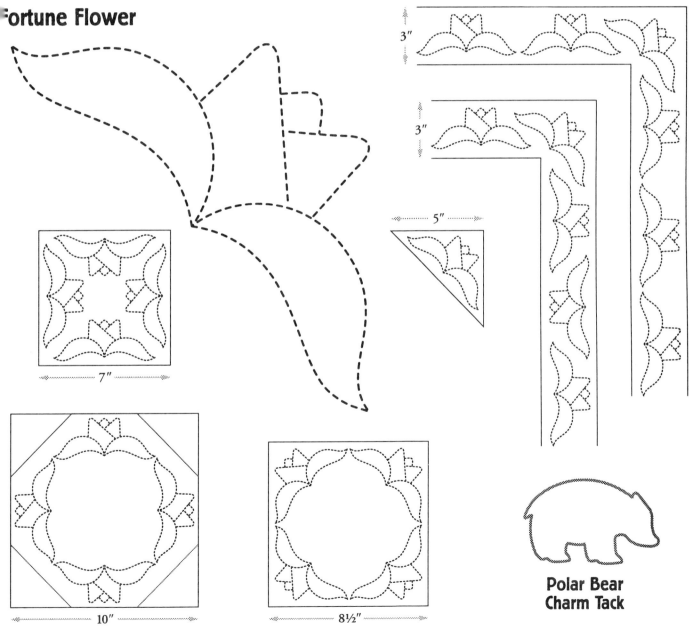

3"

3"

5"

7"

10"

8½"

**Polar Bear
Charm Tack**

Floral Spray

Arrows indicate direction for continuous-line machine quilting.

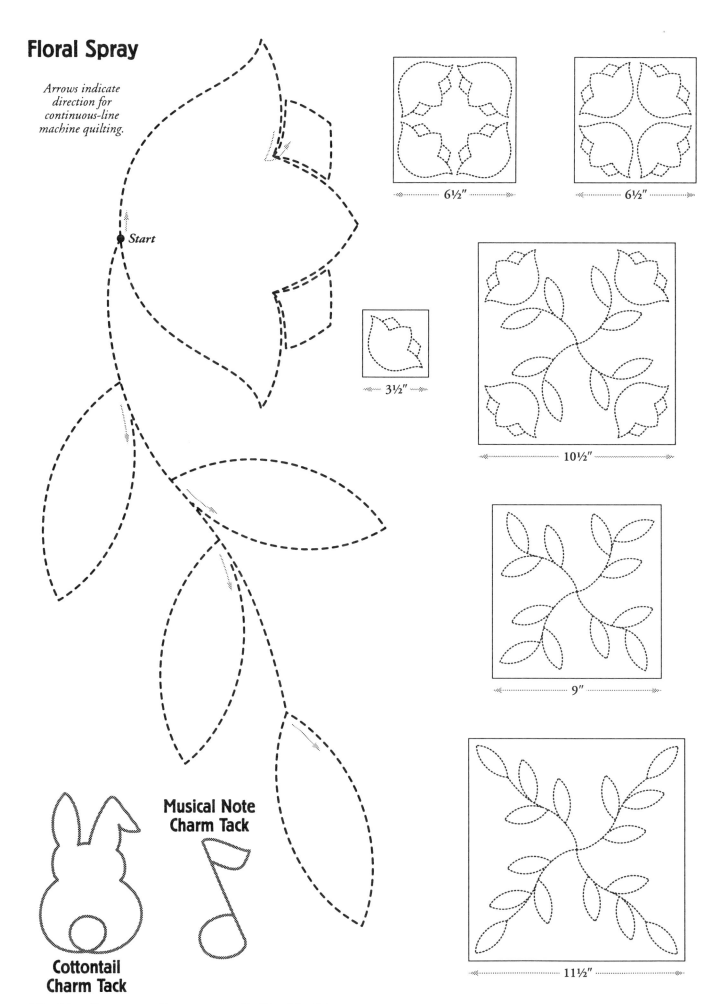

Start

6½"

6½"

3½"

10½"

9"

11½"

Musical Note Charm Tack

Cottontail Charm Tack

Floral Spray

Reversed motifs are shown in gray.

4½"

4½"

12"
(10" circle)

13½"

4½"

15"

Cabbage Rose

3½"

3½"

6"

5½"

5½"

8½"

8"

8½"

Main Street

4"

10½"

10½"

7½"

8½"

11"

Snow Blossom

Lilting Leaf

2½"

4½"

3"

4"

4"

4½"

7"

Chicken & Rooster Charm Tacks

Heart's Flower

Arrows indicate direction for continuous-line machine quilting.

3½"

3"

3"

3"   2½"

3"

3½"

5"

6"

3"

7"

3½"

11½"

9"

8"

6"

6"

Heart's Flower

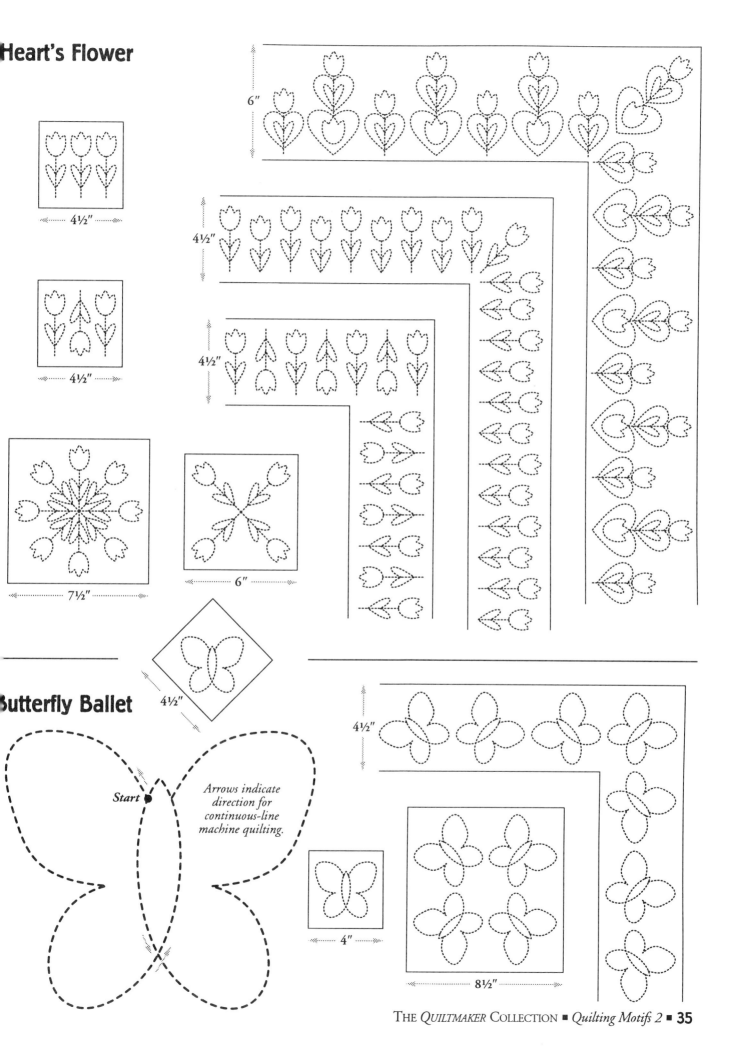

6"

4½"

4½"

4½"

4½"

7½"

6"

4½"

Butterfly Ballet

4½"

Start

Arrows indicate direction for continuous-line machine quilting.

4"

8½"

English Garden

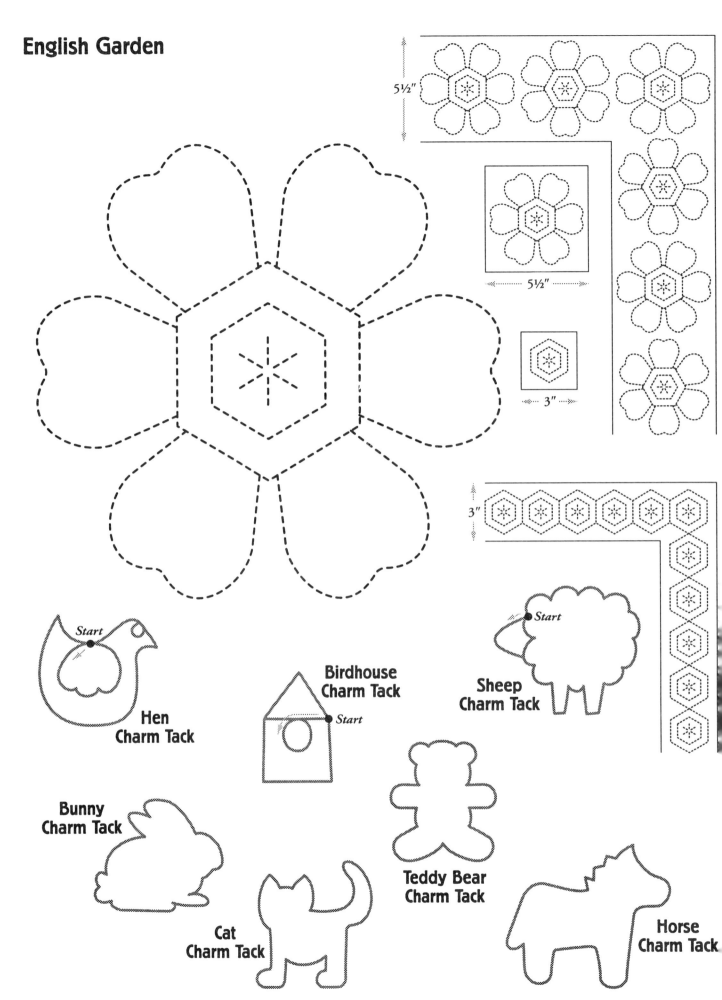

5½"

5½"

3"

3"

Hen
Charm Tack

Start

Birdhouse
Charm Tack

Start

Sheep
Charm Tack

Start

Bunny
Charm Tack

Cat
Charm Tack

Teddy Bear
Charm Tack

Horse
Charm Tack

Leaf Spray

2"

2"

3½"

5"

6"

8½"

5½"

10"

8"

8"

Evening Flower

3"

3½"

5½"

6"

Center

Place on fold and rotate to complete motif.

17"

Evening Flower

4½"

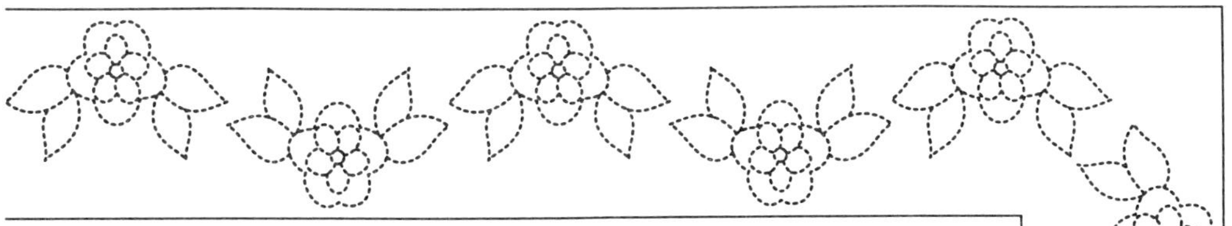

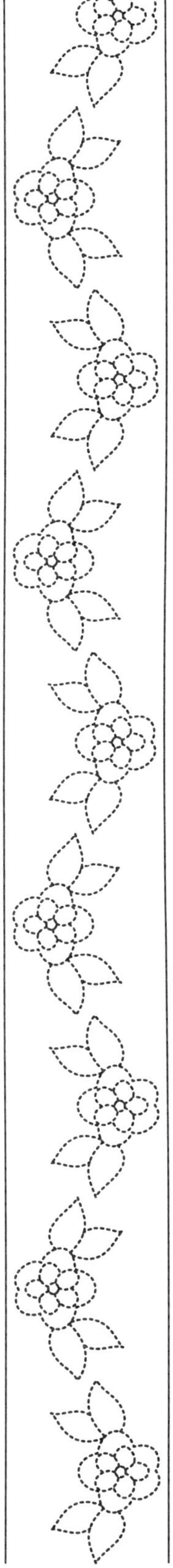

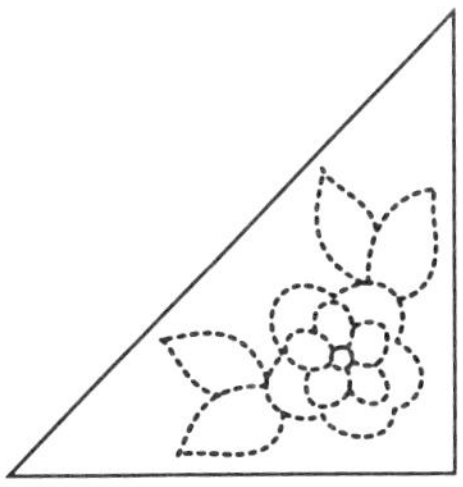

6"

12½"

12½"

8½"

10"

12½"

11"

Washington's Wreath

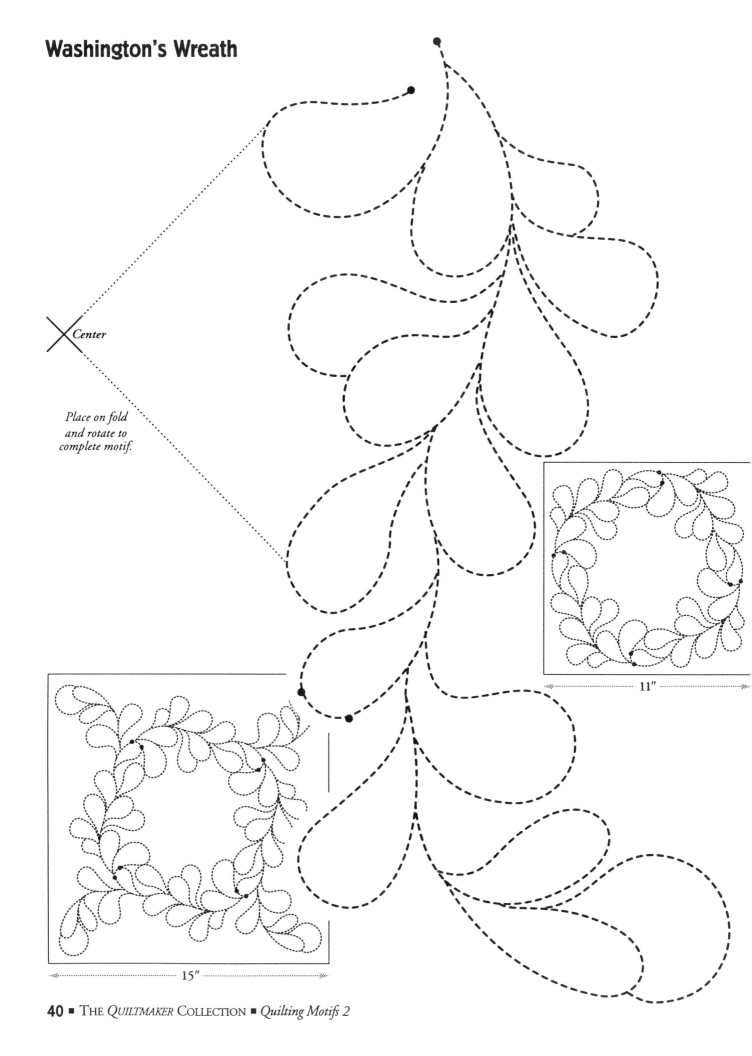

Center

*Place on fold
and rotate to
complete motif.*

11"

15"

Grapevine

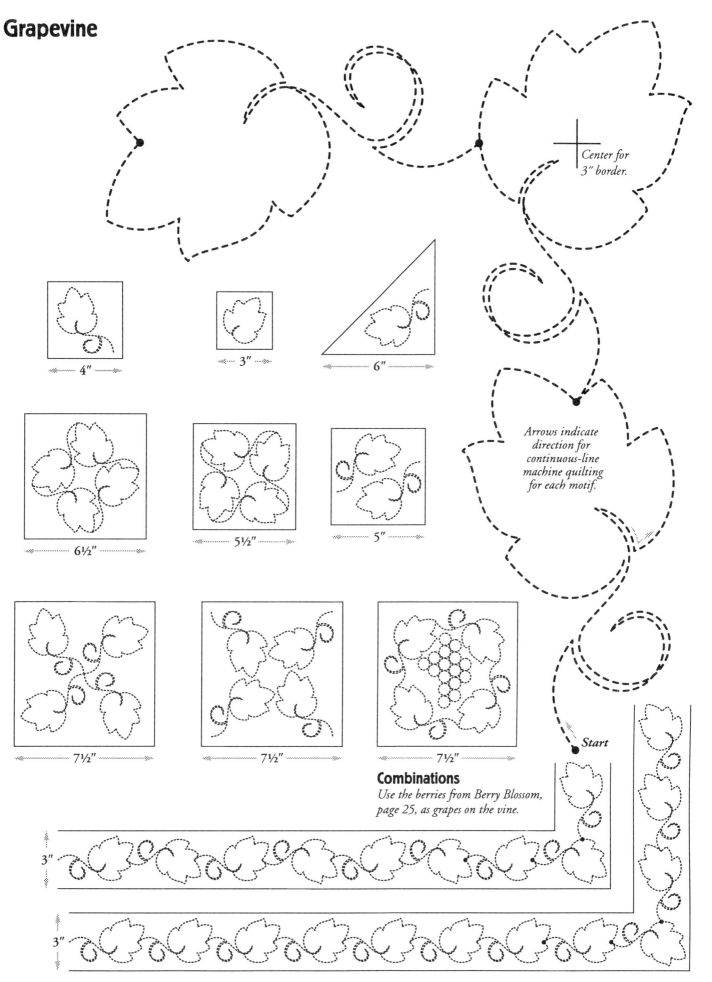

Center for 3" border.

4"

3"

6"

Arrows indicate direction for continuous-line machine quilting for each motif.

6½"

5½"

5"

7½"

7½"

7½"

Start

Combinations
Use the berries from Berry Blossom, page 25, as grapes on the vine.

3"

3"

Herbal Medley

7"

8"

8½"

3½"

3½"

3½"

5"

5"

6"

5"

Herbal Medley

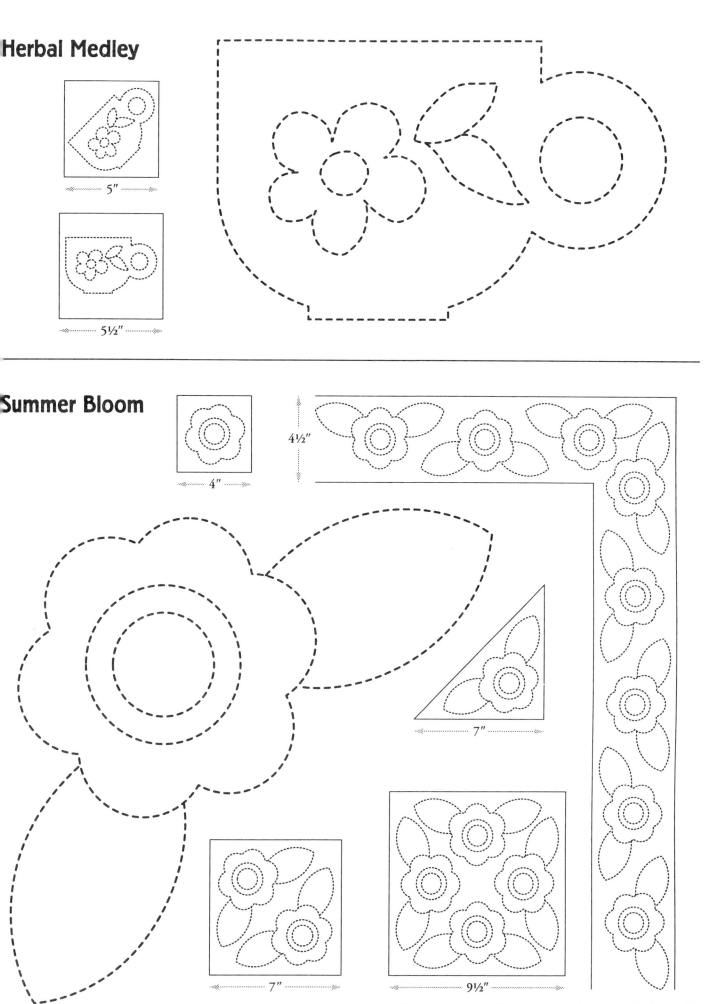

5"

5½"

Summer Bloom

4"

4½"

7"

7"

9½"

Butterfly

Maple Leaf

Leaf & Tendril

Reversed motifs are shown in gray.

4"

7½"

6"

10"

4"

14"

Iris Jubilee

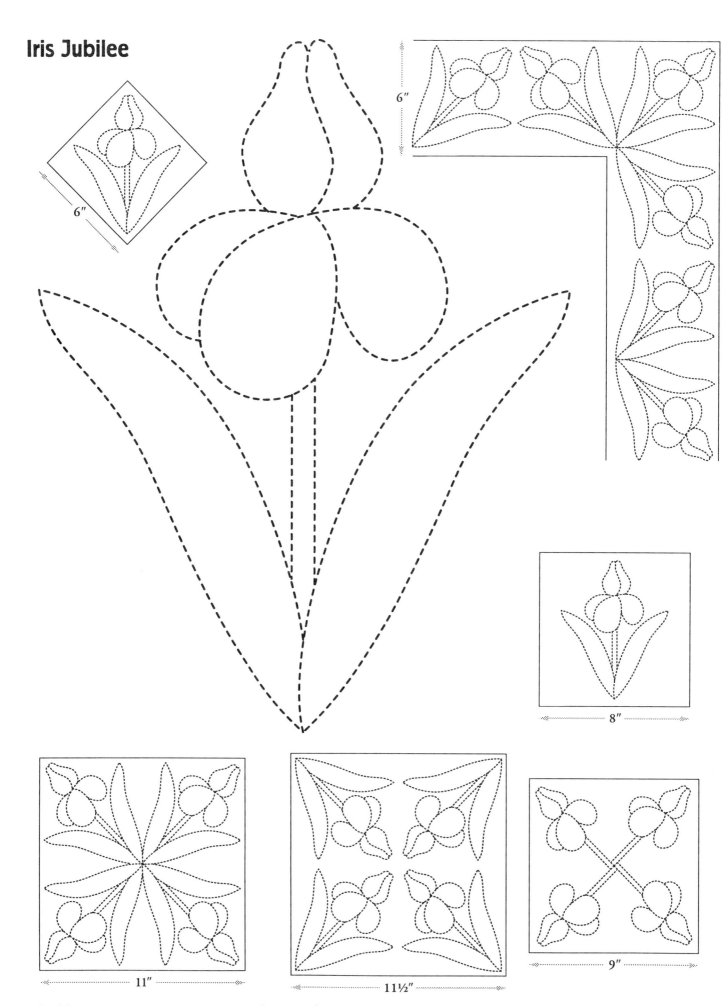

6"

6"

8"

11"

11½"

9"

Rose Beauty

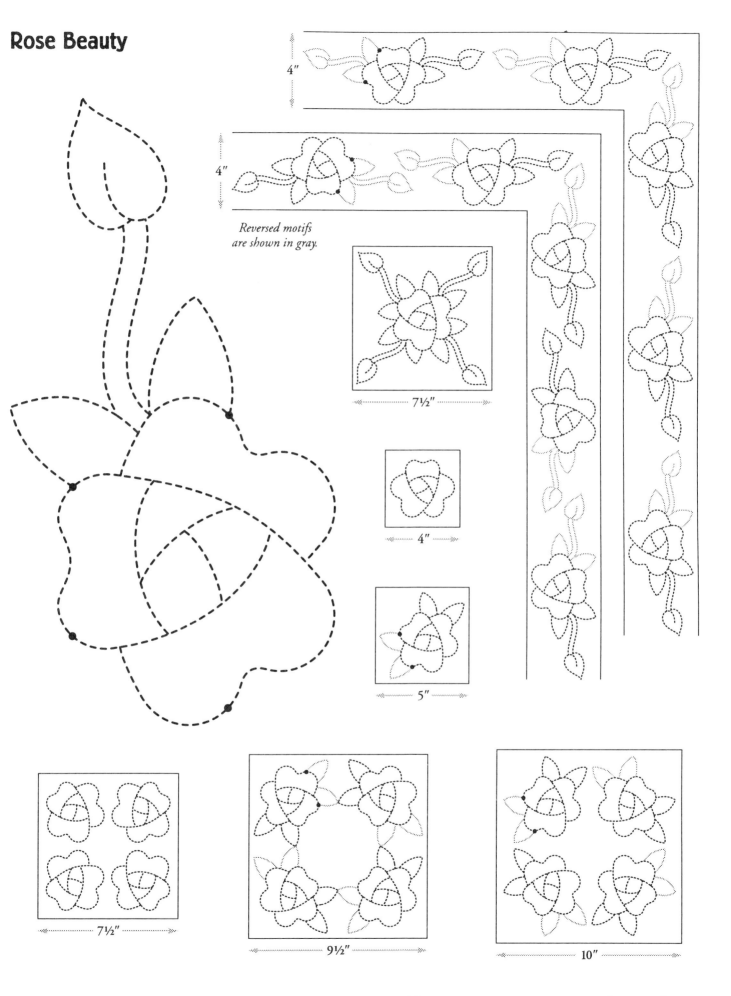

4"

4"

*Reversed motifs
are shown in gray.*

7½"

4"

5"

7½"

9½"

10"

Jaunty Jump-Ups

3½"

6½"

6"

6"

7"

6"

5½"
(4½" circle)

8½"

7"

8½"
(7" circle)

Yukon Cable

Morning's Glory

4½"

4½"

Reversed motifs are shown in gray.

6½"

7"

8"

8"

8"

Morning's Glory

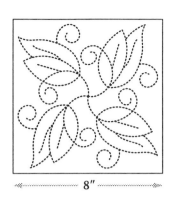

8"

11"

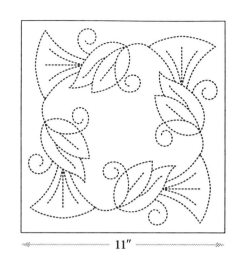

11"

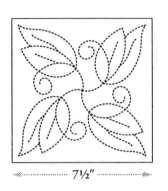

7½"

6½"

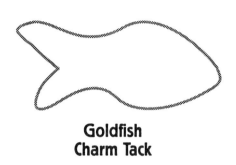

**Goldfish
Charm Tack**

Pinwheel Posey

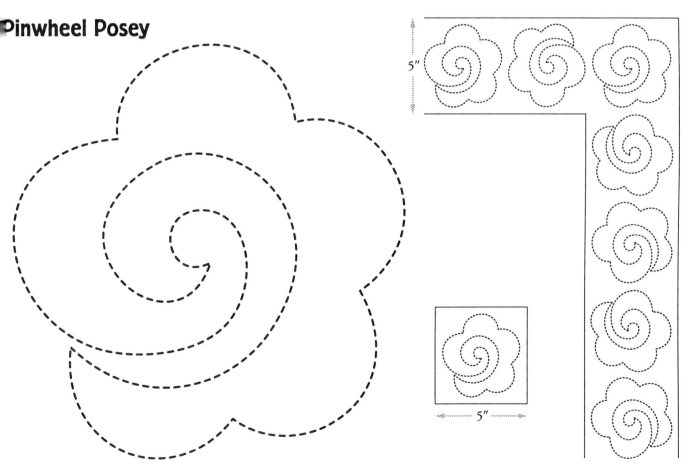

5"

5"

Harvest Bloom

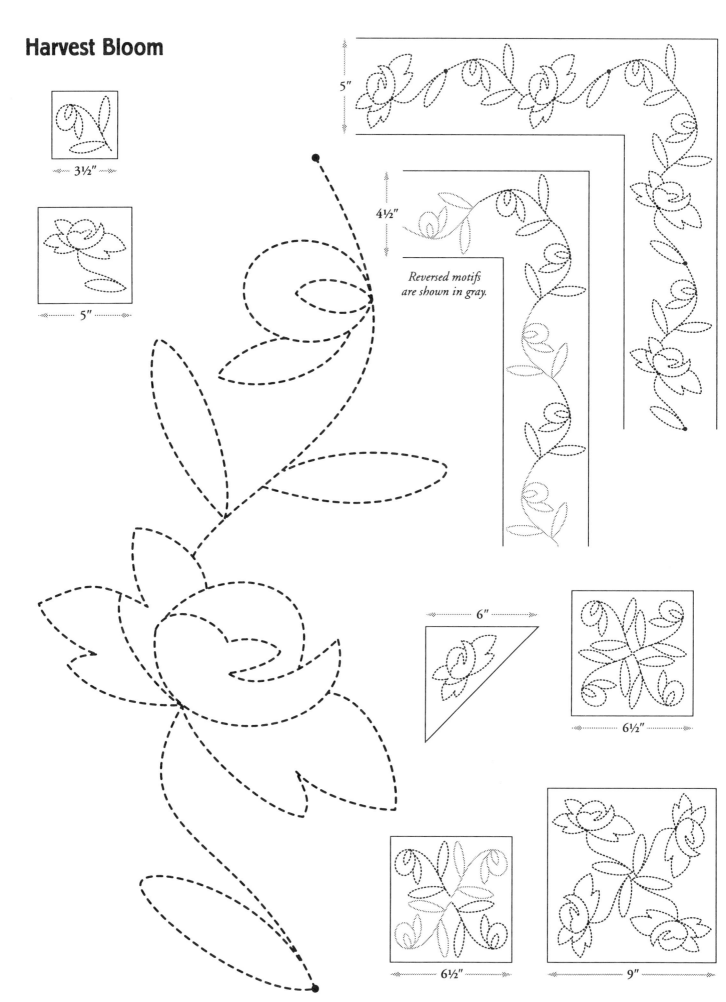

3½"

5"

5"

4½"

Reversed motifs
are shown in gray.

6"

6½"

6½"

9"

Hearts & Flowers

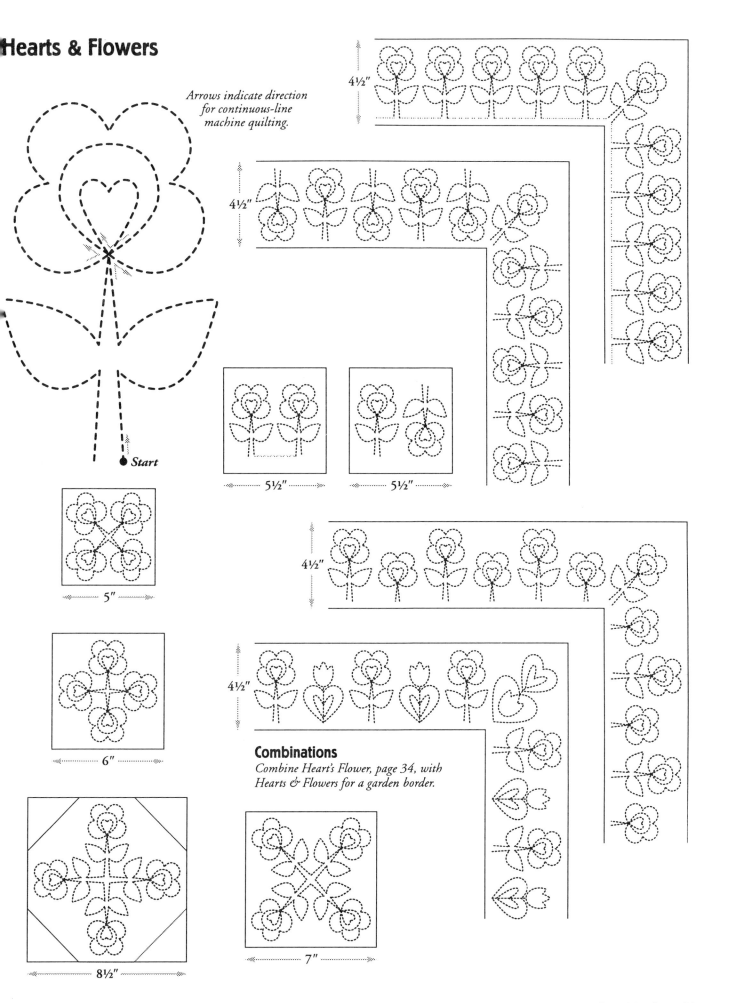

Arrows indicate direction for continuous-line machine quilting.

● *Start*

5"

6"

8½"

4½"

4½"

5½"

5½"

4½"

4½"

Combinations

Combine Heart's Flower, page 34, with Hearts & Flowers for a garden border.

7"

Silver Bells

4½"

7½"

10"

10"
(8½" circle)

9"

He-Loves-Me

Arrows indicate direction for continuous-line machine quilting.

Start

4½"

3"

3½"

5"

4½"

2"

2"

3"

9"

6½"

6½"

7"

Happy Days

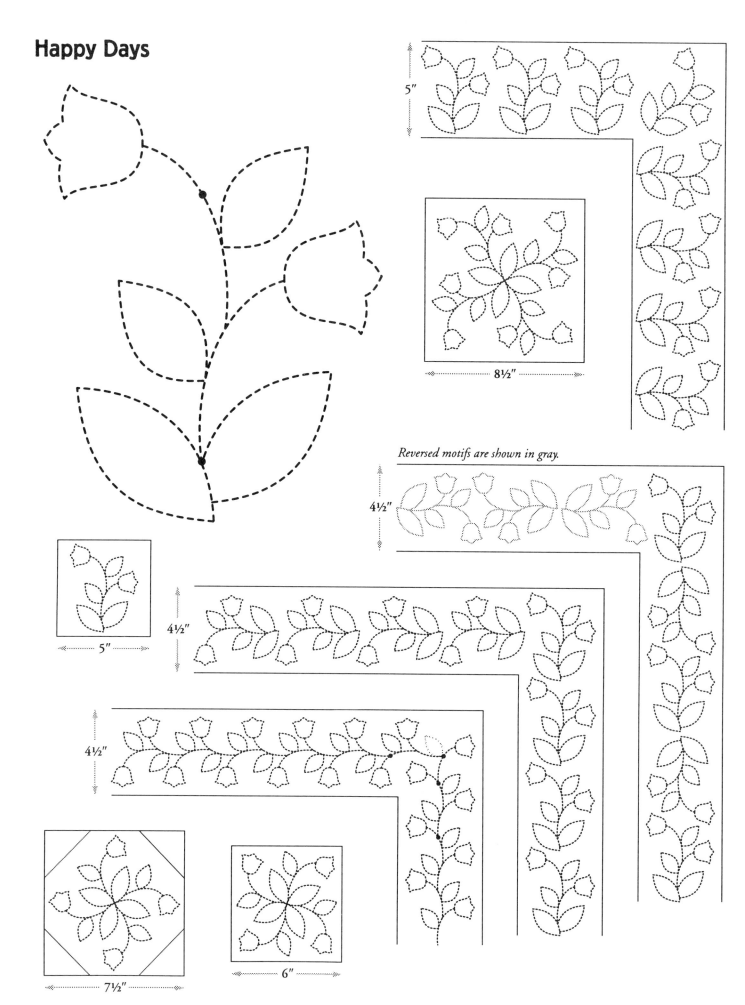

Reversed motifs are shown in gray.

Tulip Wreath

Center
Place on fold and rotate to complete motif.

3″

3″

6½″

9½″

7″

9½″

Giraffe Charm Tack

Robin Charm Tack

Butterfly Dance

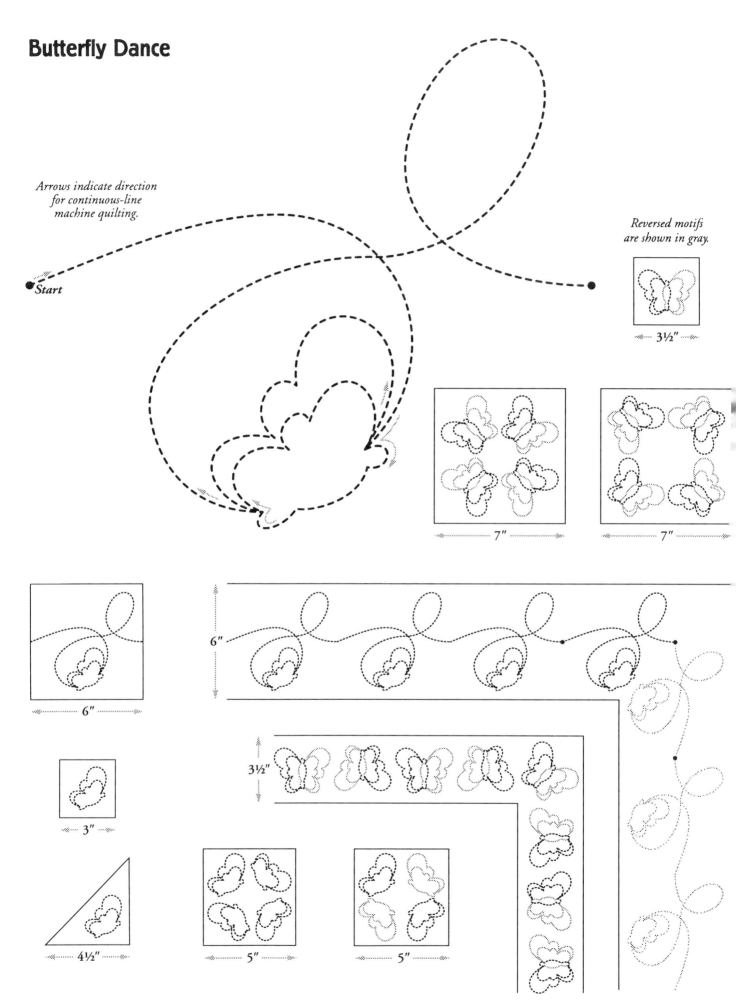

Arrows indicate direction
for continuous-line
machine quilting.

Start

Reversed motifs
are shown in gray.

3½"

7"

7"

6"

6"

3½"

3"

4½"

5"

5"

Two Bunnies

Reversed motifs are shown in gray.

5½"

8"

5½"

Best Foot Forward

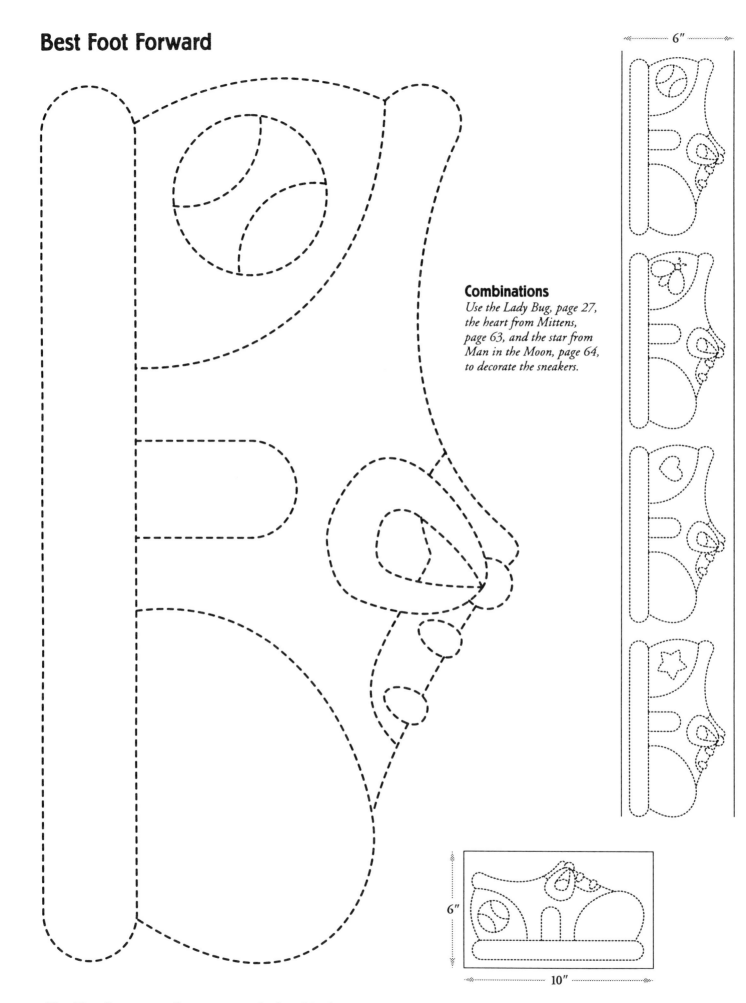

Combinations
Use the Lady Bug, page 27, the heart from Mittens, page 63, and the star from Man in the Moon, page 64, to decorate the sneakers.

6"

6"

10"

Bicycle

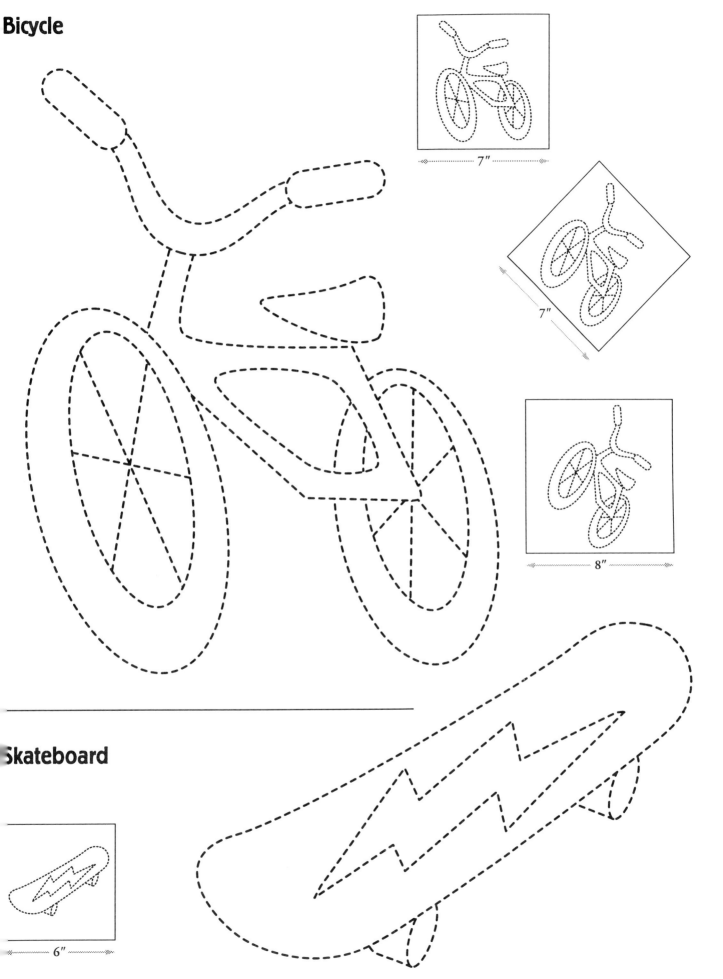

7"

7"

8"

Skateboard

6"

Kickapoo Ponies

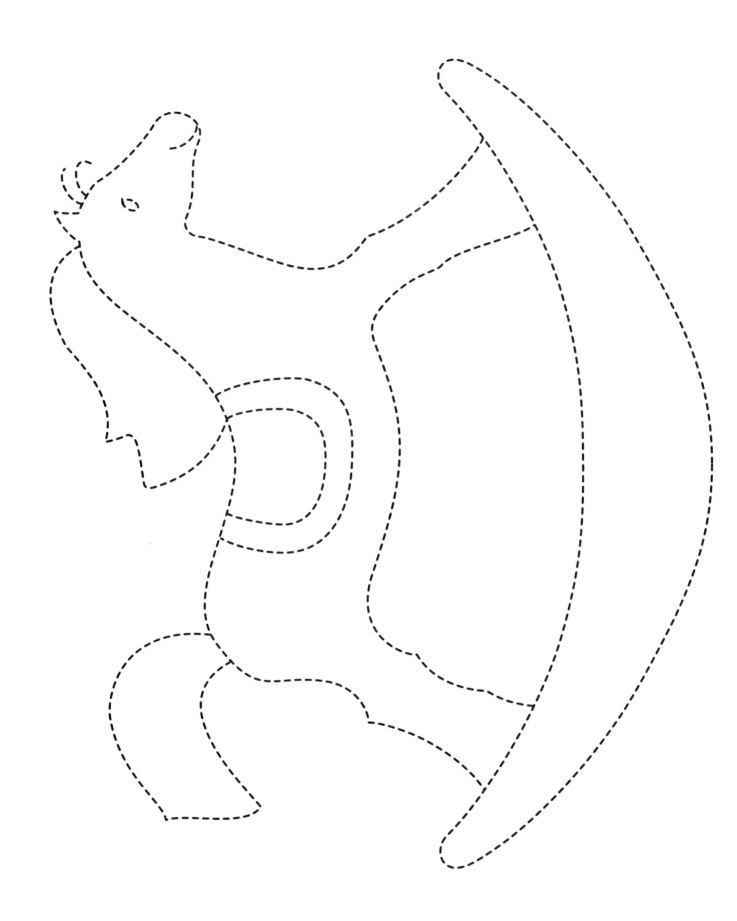

Kickapoo Ponies

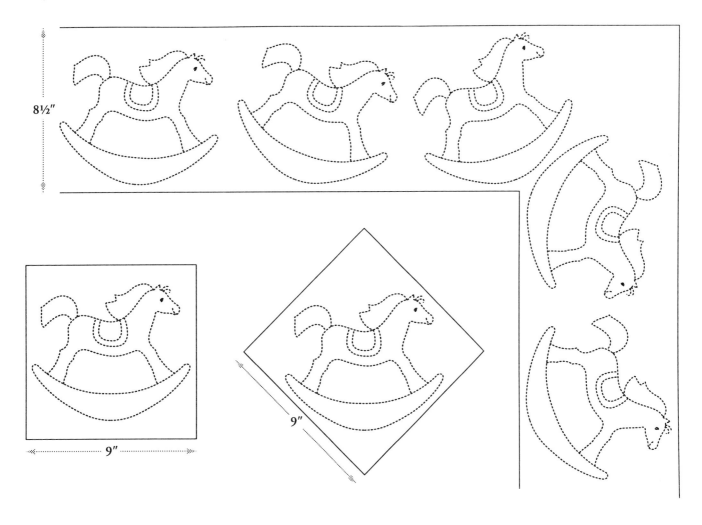

8½"

9"

9"

Mittens

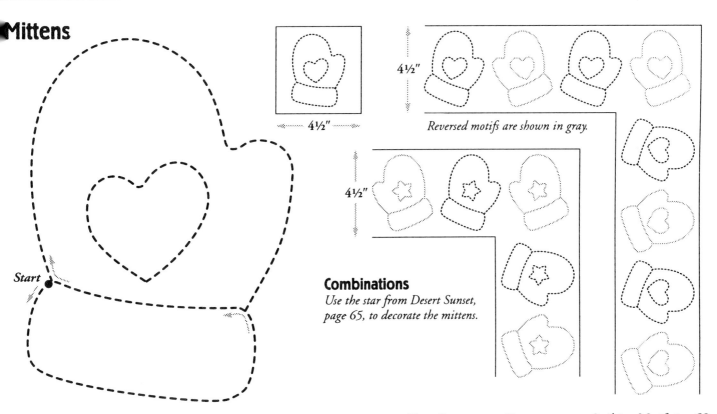

4½"

4½"

4½"

Reversed motifs are shown in gray.

Start

Combinations
Use the star from Desert Sunset, page 65, to decorate the mittens.

Man in the Moon

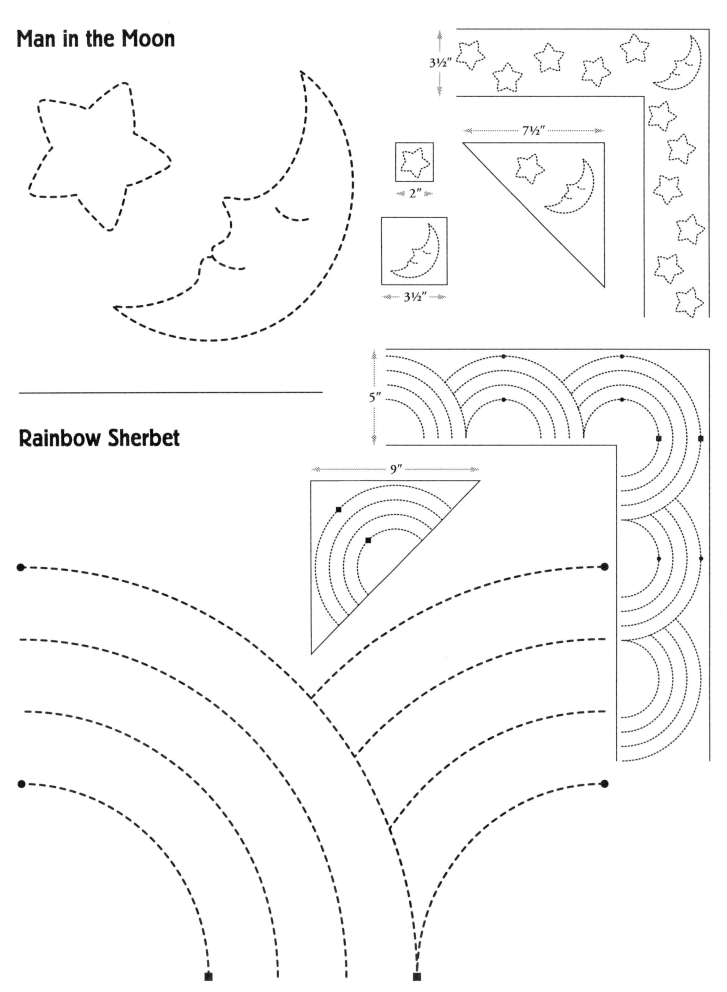

Rainbow Sherbet

Desert Sunset

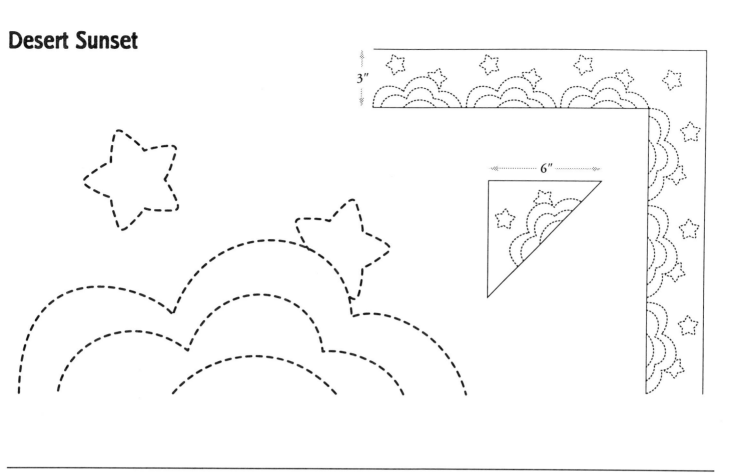

3"

6"

Rain or Shine

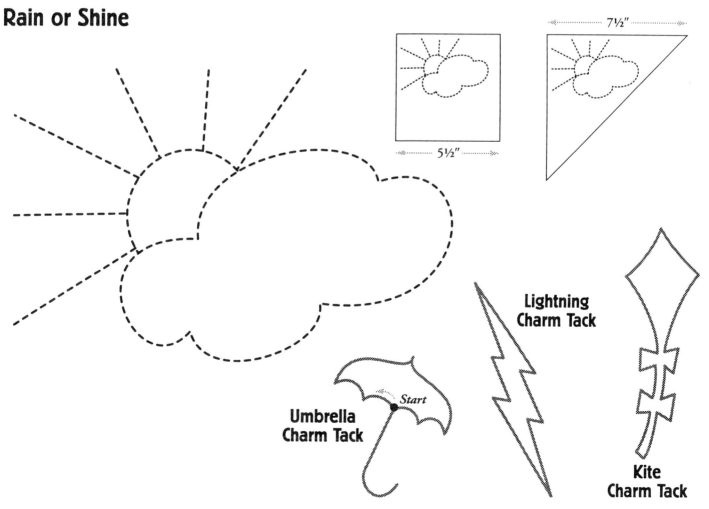

7½"

5½"

Lightning Charm Tack

Umbrella Charm Tack

Start

Kite Charm Tack

Puppy Romp

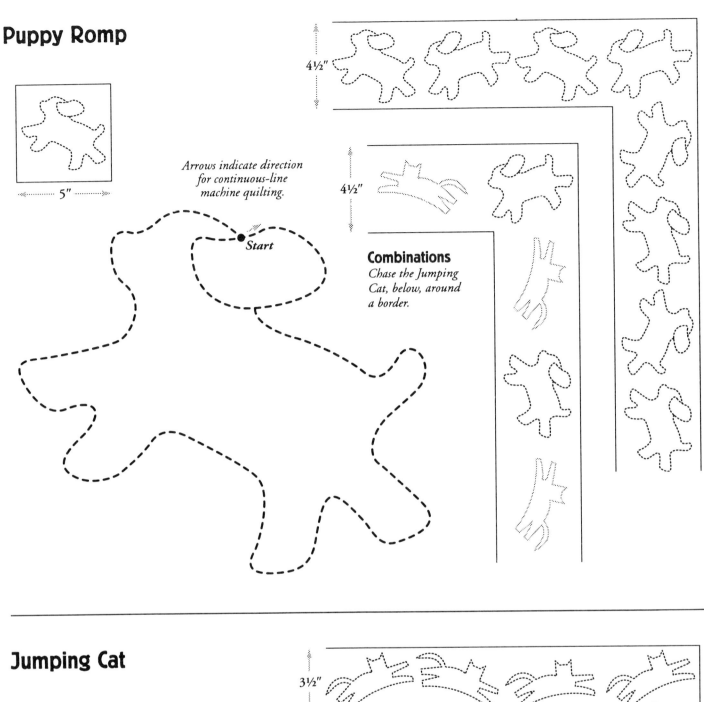

5"

4½"

4½"

Arrows indicate direction
for continuous-line
machine quilting.

Start

Combinations
Chase the Jumping
Cat, below, around
a border.

Jumping Cat

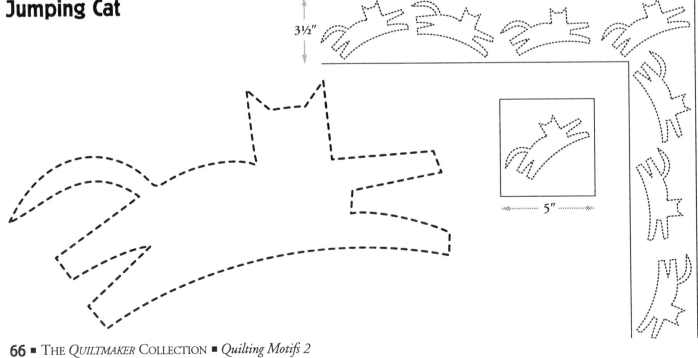

3½"

5"

Triple Scoop

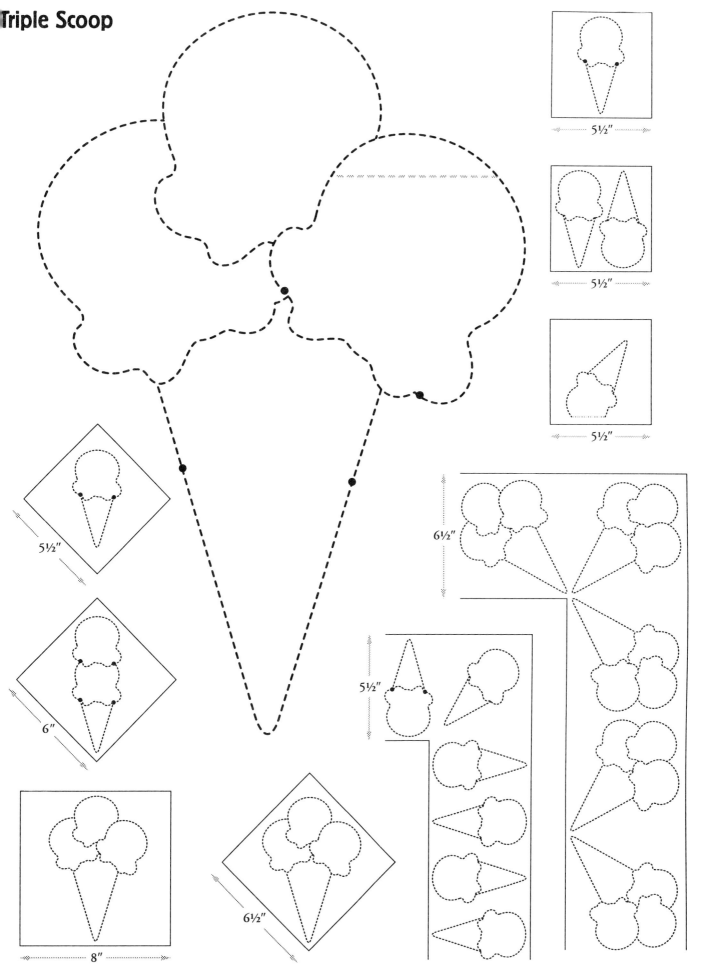

5½"

5½"

5½"

5½"

6"

8"

6½"

6½"

5½"

To the Moon

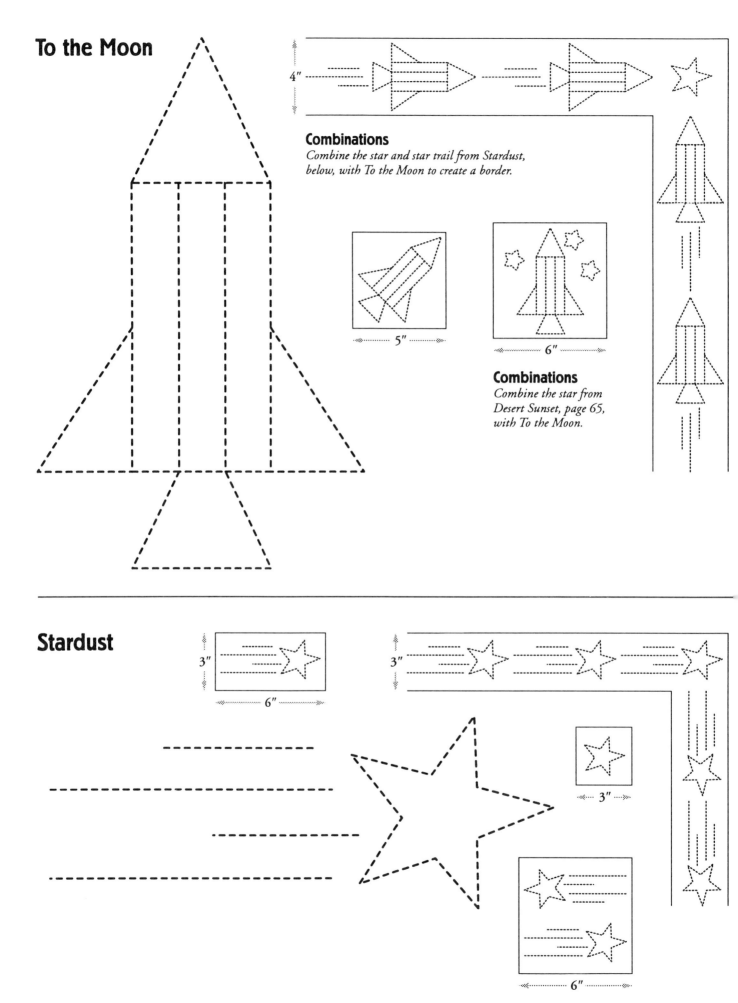

Combinations
Combine the star and star trail from Stardust, below, with To the Moon to create a border.

5"

6"

Combinations
Combine the star from Desert Sunset, page 65, with To the Moon.

4"

Stardust

3"

6"

3"

3"

6"

Castle

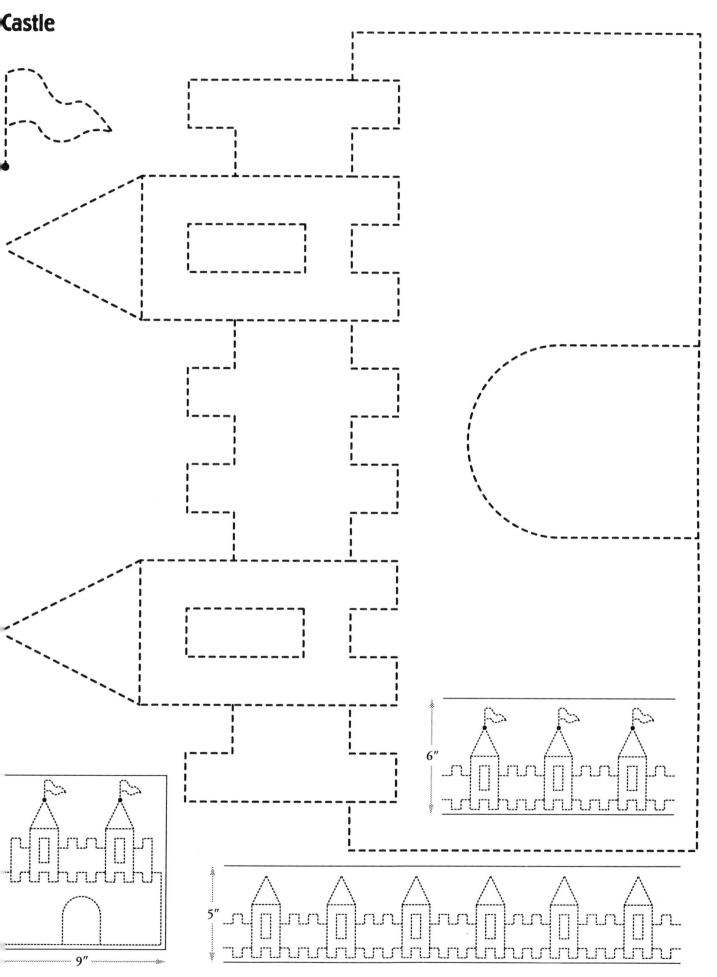

King/Wizard

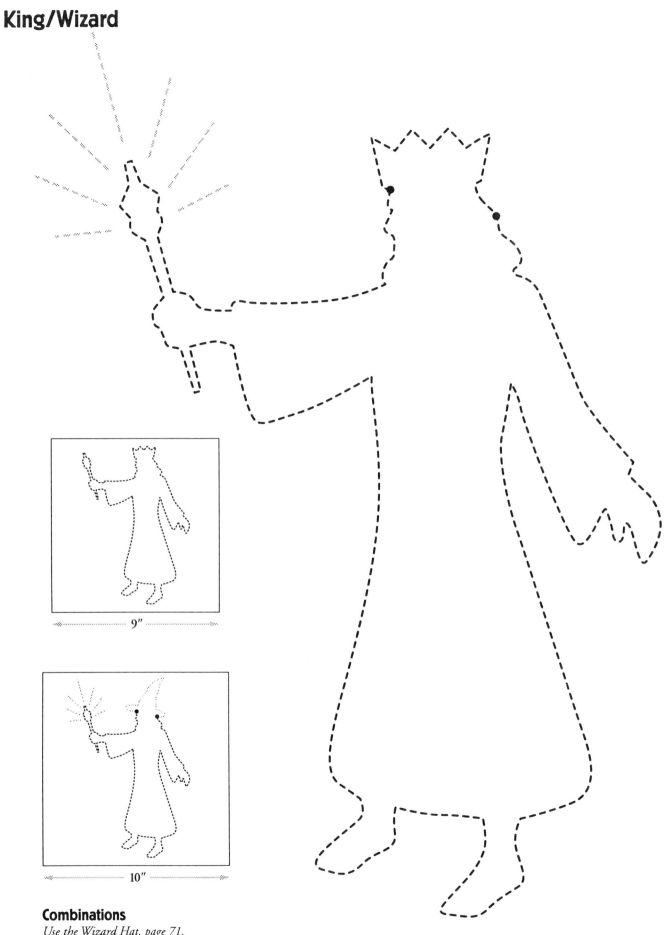

9"

10"

Combinations
*Use the Wizard Hat, page 71,
to turn the King into a Wizard.*

Princess/Owl/Wizard Hat

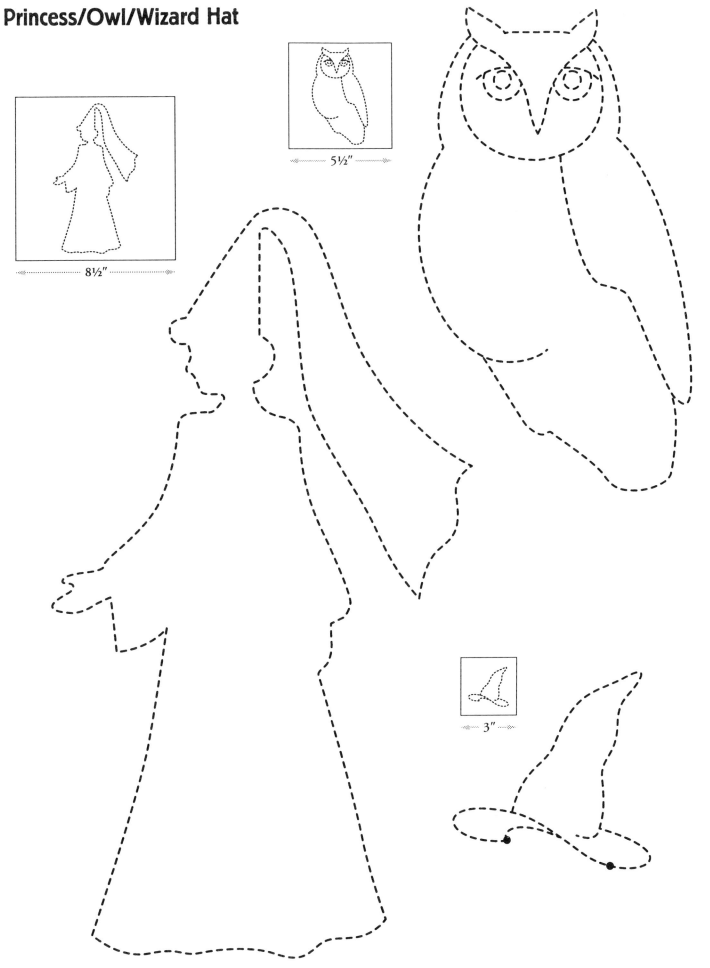

8½"

5½"

3"

Flying Dragon

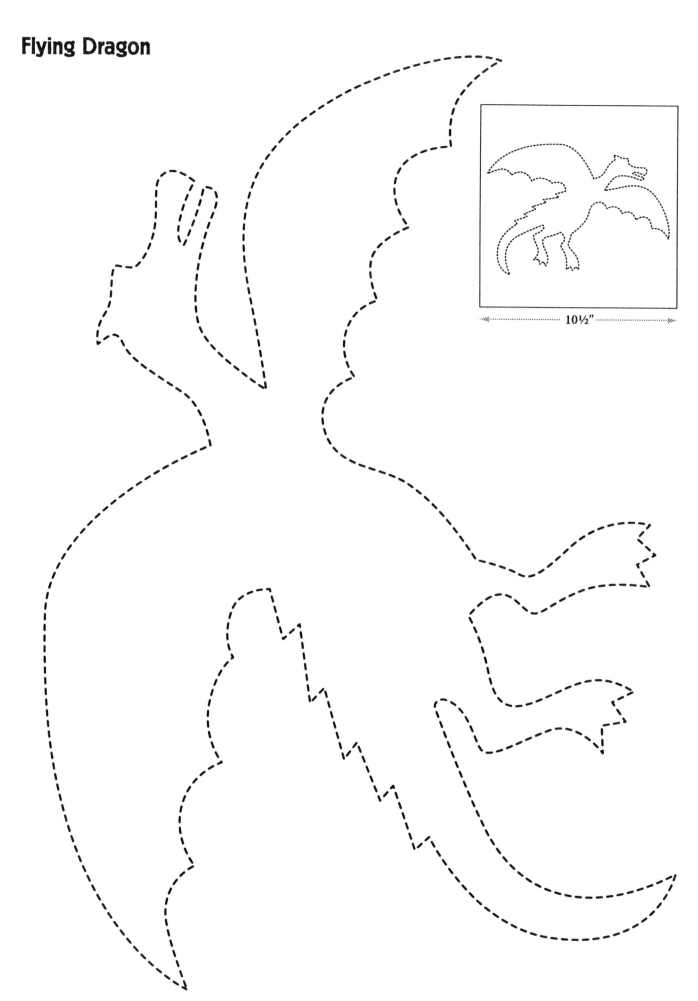

10½″

Sea Serpent/Knight

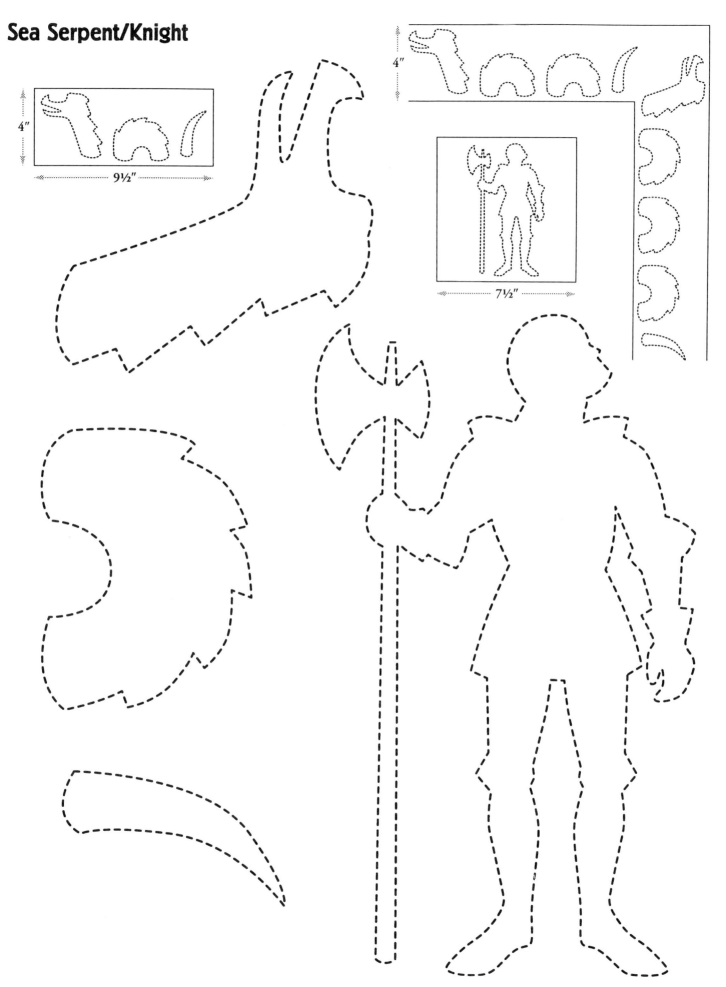

4"

9½"

4"

7½"

Unicorn/Horse

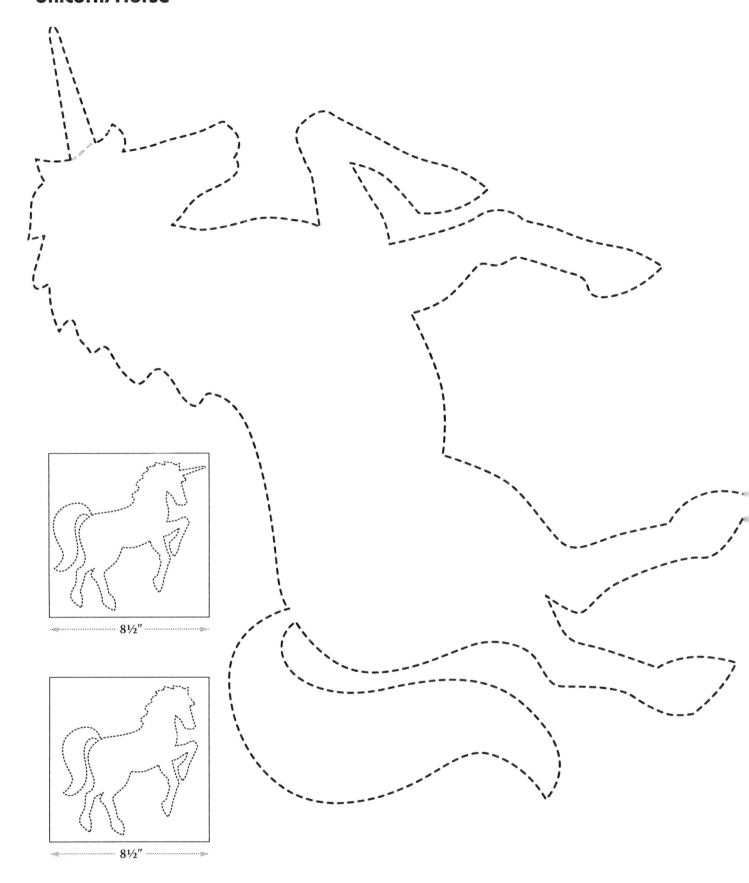

8½"

8½"

Dolphin Bay

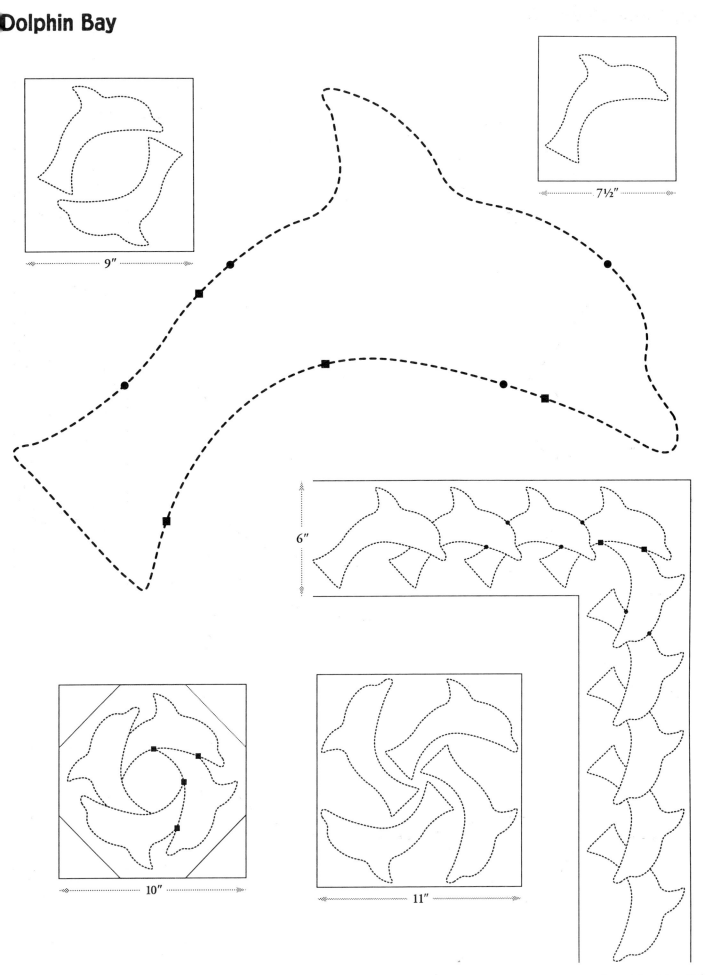

9"

7½"

6"

10"

11"

Elephants on Parade

Duck Stroll

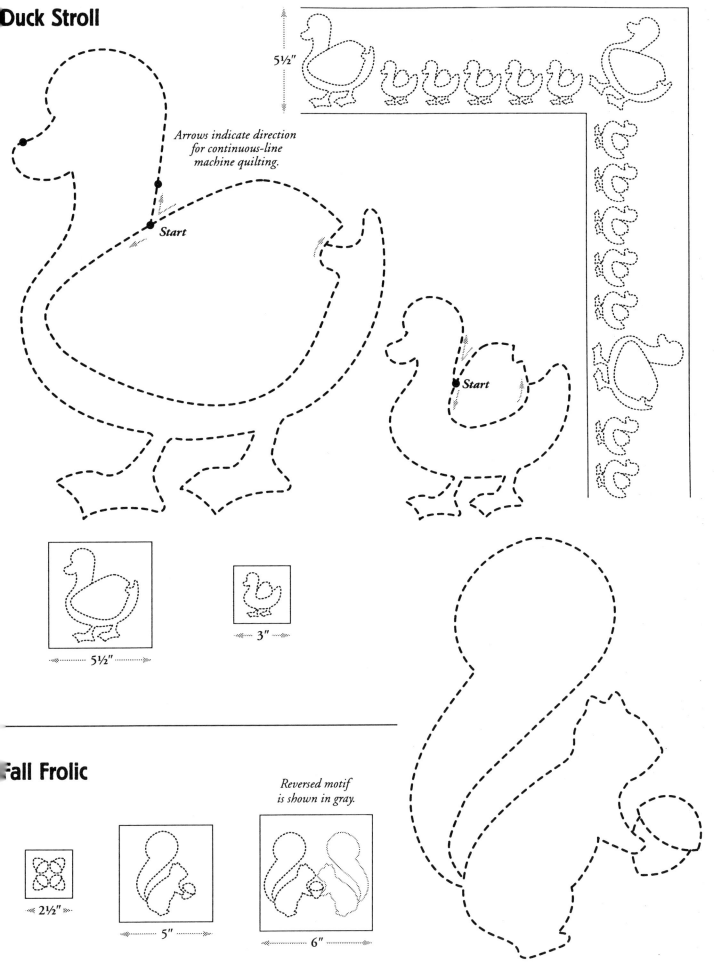

Arrows indicate direction for continuous-line machine quilting.

Start

5½"

Start

5½"

3"

Fall Frolic

Reversed motif is shown in gray.

2½"

5"

6"

Peace Sign

Combinations
*Combine the '60s era designs
from these two pages.*

5"

5"

5"

Happy Face

5"

5"

Groovy Flowers

4½"

4½"

4½"

7"

Psychedelic Swirls

5"

9"

5"

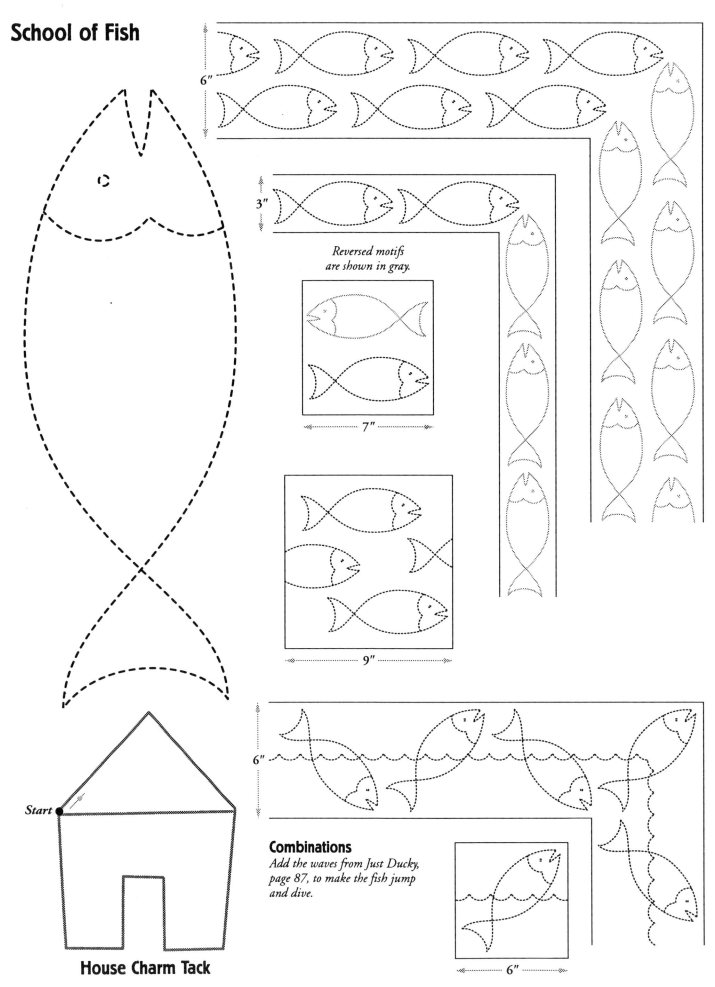

School of Fish

6"

3"

Reversed motifs
are shown in gray.

7"

9"

Start

House Charm Tack

6"

Combinations

Add the waves from Just Ducky,
page 87, to make the fish jump
and dive.

6"

Garden Fairy

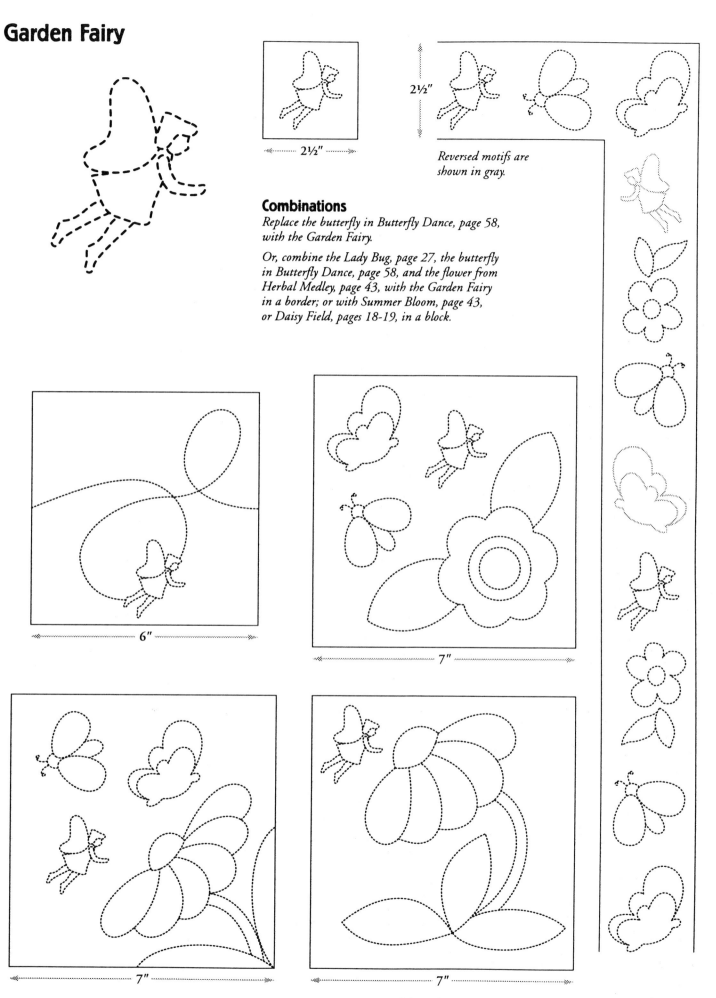

2½"

2½"

Reversed motifs are shown in gray.

Combinations
Replace the butterfly in Butterfly Dance, page 58, with the Garden Fairy.

Or, combine the Lady Bug, page 27, the butterfly in Butterfly Dance, page 58, and the flower from Herbal Medley, page 43, with the Garden Fairy in a border; or with Summer Bloom, page 43, or Daisy Field, pages 18-19, in a block.

6"

7"

7"

7"

Raccoon Balloons

10½"

7½"

Raccoon Balloons

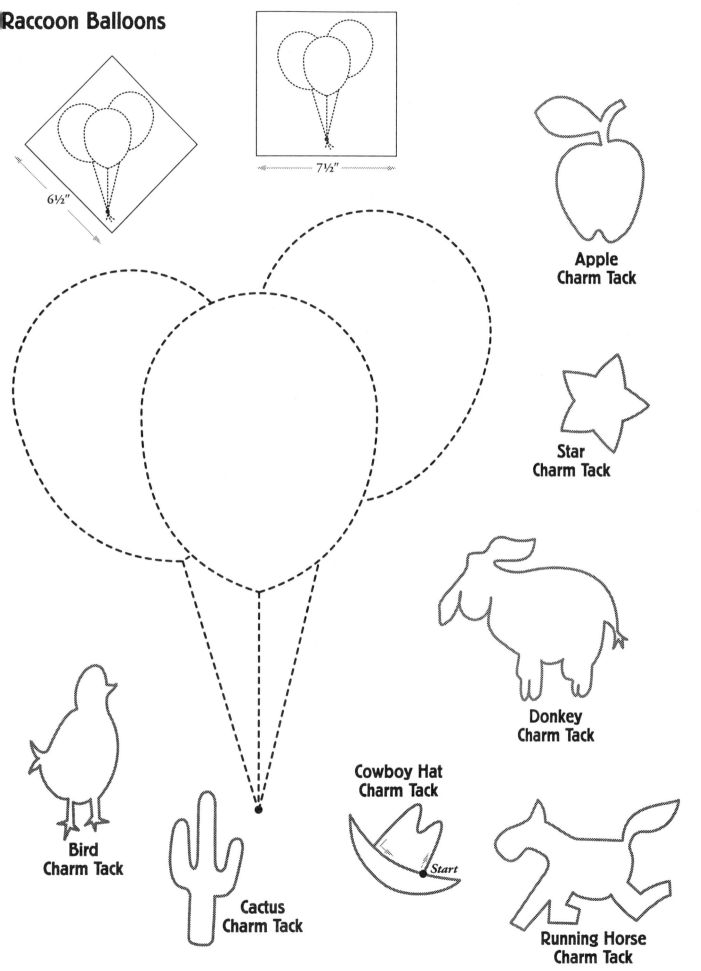

6½"

7½"

Apple Charm Tack

Star Charm Tack

Donkey Charm Tack

Bird Charm Tack

Cactus Charm Tack

Cowboy Hat Charm Tack

Start

Running Horse Charm Tack

Baby Birds

3½"

4½"

3½"

Teddy Bear

2"

4½"

4"

2"

Reversed motifs are shown in gray.

2"

4"

Penguin on Ice

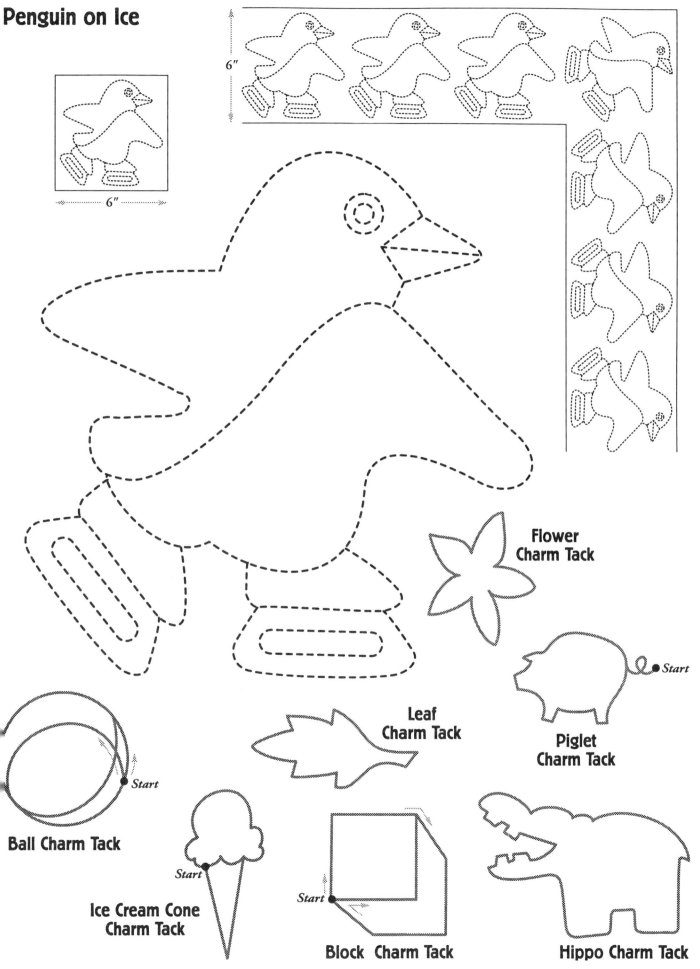

6"

6"

Flower Charm Tack

Leaf Charm Tack

Piglet Charm Tack

Start

Ball Charm Tack

Start

Ice Cream Cone Charm Tack

Start

Block Charm Tack

Start

Hippo Charm Tack

Sheriff's Badge

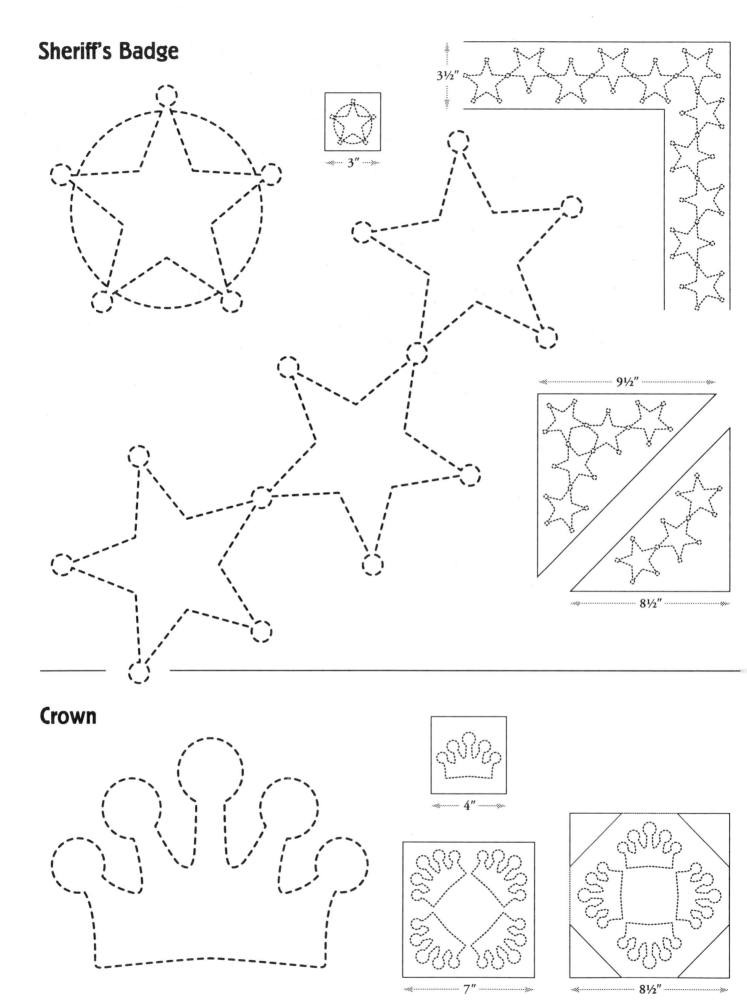

3"

3½"

9½"

8½"

Crown

4"

7"

8½"

Just Ducky

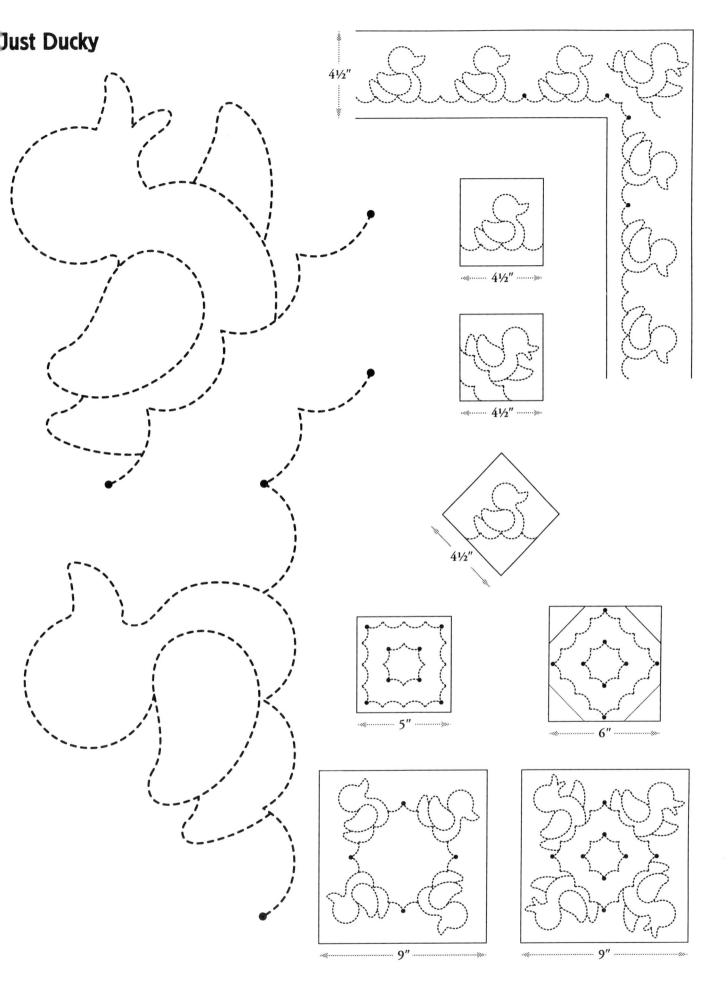

4½"

4½"

4½"

4½"

5"

6"

9"

9"

Cover Quilt Pattern

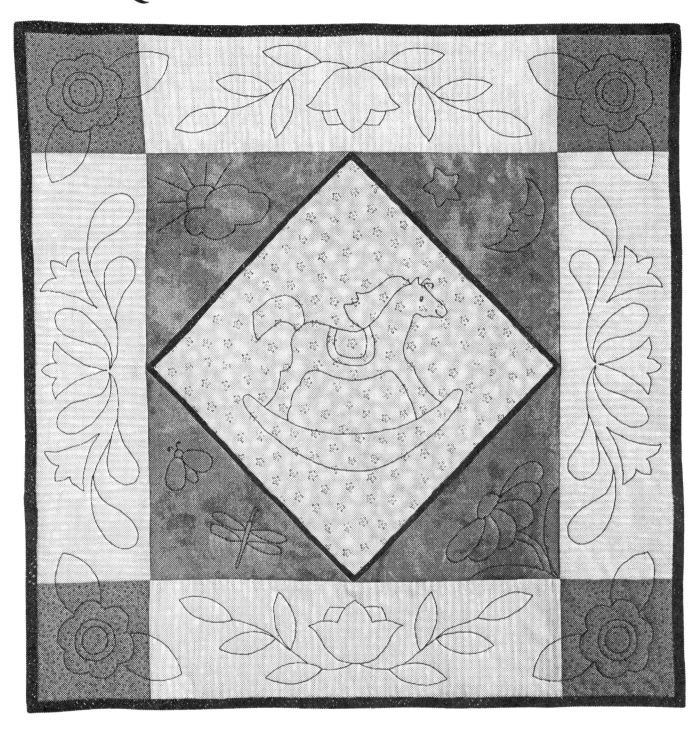

If you just can't wait to try out some of the motifs in this book and you don't have a current project for them, how about making your own version of the quilt shown on the cover? You can create one just like ours, or you can substitute other motifs that caught your eye. The quilt top goes together so easily that you'll be quilting in no time!

🧵 Easy

QUILT SIZE:	Wall Quilt
	24¾"x 24¾"
YARDAGE: (44" fabric)	
Light Green Print........	⅜ yard
	1 A
Blue Print...............	⅓ yard
	4 B
Yellow Print ◆...........	⅓ yard
	4 C
Pink Print..............	¼ yard
	4 D
Dark Blue Print........	⅓ yard
folded border strips	4 at 1"x 12½"
double-fold binding	3 at 2¼"x 40"
Lining..................	⅞ yard
panel	1 at 29"x 29"
sleeve	1 at 9"x 24"
Batting.................	29"x 29"

◆ If stripe runs selvedge to selvedge, you'll need ½ yard.

Preparing the Folded Border

Fold and press each dark blue border strip the long way, *wrong* sides together, forming strips ½" x 12½". Align the long raw edges of one folded border strip to one side of A. Baste ⅛" in from the raw edges and trim the extra length. Baste the remaining border strips to the other 3 sides, overlapping ends as needed.

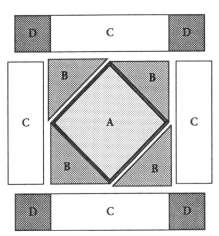

Quilt Assembly

Making the Quilt Top

Referring to the assembly diagram, piece the quilt top, sandwiching the folded border between A and B's as you construct the center portion. Press seam allowances away from the center.

Quilting

The motifs used for this quilt are Kickapoo Ponies, page 62; Rain or Shine, 65; Man in the Moon, 64; Daisy Field, 18; Dragonfly, 21; Lady Bug, 27; Floral Spray, 28; Summer Bloom, 43; and Evening Trumpet, 10. If you'd like to use different motifs, look in the Size Index under 9½" block for patch A and the 4½" border category for border designs.

Referring to the quilting diagram, trace the motifs as shown. If you plan to use tracing paper for marking, trace the motifs on paper.

Layer the lining, batting and quilt top and baste the layers together.

Quilt in the ditch along the folded border seam line. Quilt the marked motifs.

Finishing

Enclose the edges with binding and add a sleeve to the lining.

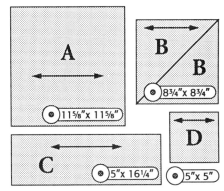

Align arrows with lengthwise or crosswise grain of fabric.

Quilting Motif Placement

Index

Size Index

Squares

2"
Man in the Moon, 64
Snow Blossom, 32
Teddy Bear, 84

2½"
Fall Frolic, 77
Garden Fairy, 81
Granny Smith's, 15
Heart's Flower, 34
Lady Bug, 27
Snow Blossom, 32
Springtime, 22

3"
Butterfly Dance, 58
Duck Stroll, 77
English Garden, 36
Evening Flower, 38
Grapevine, 41
Heart's Flower, 34
Sheriff's Badge, 86
Springtime, 22
Stardust, 68
Wizard Hat, 71
Yukon Cable, 49

3½"
Baby Birds, 84
Barn Swallow, 26
Berry Blossom, 25
Butterfly Dance, 58
Celestial, 12
Dragonfly, 21
Evening Flower, 38
Floral Spray, 28
Harvest Bloom, 52
Heart's Flower, 34
Herbal Medley, 42
Honeybee, 19
Jaunty Jump-Ups, 48
Man in the Moon, 64
Snow Blossom, 32

4"
Autumn Leaves, 26
Butterfly Ballet, 35
Celebration, 17
Crown, 86
Graceful Vine, 25
Grapevine, 41
Leaf & Tendril, 45
Lilting Leaf, 33
Rose Beauty, 47
Snow Blossom, 32
Summer Bloom, 43

Teddy Bear, 84
Yukon Cable, 49

4½"
Baby Birds, 84
Butterfly Ballet, 35
Dogwood, 20
Groovy Flowers, 79
Heart's Flower, 35
He-Loves-Me, 55
Just Ducky, 87
Lady Bug, 27
Lilting Leaf, 33
Maple Leaf, 44
Mittens, 63
Silver Bells, 54
Snow Blossom, 32
Springtime, 22
Teddy Bear, 84

5"
Butterfly, 44
Butterfly Dance, 58
Celtic Chain, 16
Fall Frolic, 77
Fluttering Leaves, 20
Graceful Vine, 25
Granny Smith's, 15
Grapevine, 41
Happy Days, 56
Happy Face, 78
Harvest Bloom, 52
Hearts & Flowers, 53
Heart's Flower, 34
Herbal Medley, 42-43
Jumping Cat, 66
Just Ducky, 87
Leaf Spray, 37
Peace Sign, 78
Pinwheel Posey, 51
Puppy Romp, 66
Psychedelic Swirls, 79
Rose Beauty, 47
Springtime, 22
To the Moon, 68

5½"
Cabbage Rose, 30
Duck Stroll, 77
English Garden, 36
Evening Flower, 38
Evening Trumpet, 11
Grapevine, 41
Hearts & Flowers, 53
Herbal Medley, 43
Jaunty Jump-Ups, 48
Leaf Spray, 37
Owl, 71
Rain or Shine, 65
Rondo, 23
Snow Blossom, 32

Triple Scoop, 67
Two Bunnies, 59

6"
Barn Swallow, 26
Butterfly, 44
Butterfly Dance, 58
Celestial, 12
Dragonfly, 21
Evening Flower, 38
Fall Frolic, 77
Garden Fairy, 81
Happy Days, 56
Hearts & Flowers, 53
Heart's Flower, 34-35
Herbal Medley, 42
Honeybee, 19
Iris Jubilee, 46
Jaunty Jump-Ups, 48
Just Ducky, 87
Leaf Spray, 37
Lilac Leaf, 13
Penguin on Ice, 85
School of Fish, 80
Skateboard, 61
Snow Blossom, 32
Stardust, 68
To the Moon, 68
Triple Scoop, 67

6½"
Berry Blossom, 25
Celebration, 17
Floral Spray, 28
Granny Smith's, 15
Grapevine, 41
Harvest Bloom, 52
He-Loves-Me, 55
Honeybee, 19
Jaunty Jump-Ups, 48
Lilac Leaf, 13
Morning's Glory, 50-51
Raccoon Balloons, 83
Triple Scoop, 67

7"
Autumn Leaves, 26
Berry Blossom, 25
Bicycle, 61
Butterfly Dance, 58
Celtic Chain, 16
Crown, 86
Daisy Field, 18-19
Fluttering Leaves, 20
Fortune Flower, 27
Garden Fairy, 81
Groovy Flowers, 79
Hearts & Flowers, 53
He-Loves-Me, 55
Herbal Medley, 42
Jaunty Jump-Ups, 48

Lilting Leaf, 33
Morning's Glory, 50
Rondo, 23
School of Fish, 80
Summer Bloom, 43
Tulip Wreath, 57

7½"
Celebration, 17
Dolphin Bay, 75
Fluttering Leaves, 20
Granny Smith's, 15
Grapevine, 41
Happy Days, 56
Heart's Flower, 35
Knight, 73
Leaf & Tendril, 45
Main Street, 31
Morning's Glory, 51
Raccoon Balloons, 82-83
Rondo, 23
Rose Beauty, 47
Silver Bells, 54

8"
Bicycle, 61
Cabbage Rose, 30
Celestial, 12
Celtic Chain, 16
Evening Trumpet, 11
Heart's Flower, 34
Herbal Medley, 42
Iris Jubilee, 46
Leaf Spray, 37
Lilac Leaf, 13
Morning's Glory, 50-51
Triple Scoop, 67
Two Bunnies, 59
Winding Way, 14

8½"
Butterfly Ballet, 35
Cabbage Rose, 30
Crown, 86
Evening Flower, 39
Evening Trumpet, 11
Fortune Flower, 27
Happy Days, 56
Hearts & Flowers, 53
Herbal Medley, 42
Horse, 74
Jaunty Jump-Ups, 48
Leaf Spray, 37
Lilac Leaf, 13
Main Street, 31
Maple Leaf, 44
Princess, 71
Unicorn, 74
Winding Way, 14

9"
Bamboo, 21
Castle, 69
Dolphin Bay, 75
Floral Spray, 28
Harvest Bloom, 52
Heart's Flower, 34
He-Loves-Me, 55
Iris Jubilee, 46
Just Ducky, 87
Kickapoo Ponies, 63
King, 70
Lilac Leaf, 13
Psychedelic Swirls, 79
School of Fish, 80
Silver Bells, 54

9½"
Celebration, 17
Evening Trumpet, 11
Rose Beauty, 47
Summer Bloom, 43
Tulip Wreath, 57

10"
Daisy Field, 18
Dolphin Bay, 75
Elephants on Parade, 76
Evening Flower, 39
Evening Trumpet, 11
Fortune Flower, 27
Leaf & Tendril, 45
Leaf Spray, 37
Rondo, 23
Rose Beauty, 47
Silver Bells, 54
Wizard, 70 (variation)

10½"
Floral Spray, 28
Flying Dragon, 72
Lilac Leaf, 13
Main Street, 31
Raccoon Balloons, 82

11"
Dolphin Bay, 75
Evening Flower, 39
Evening Trumpet, 11
Fluttering Leaves, 20
Iris Jubilee, 46
Main Street, 31
Morning's Glory, 51
Washington's Wreath, 40

11½"
Floral Spray, 28
Iris Jubilee, 46
Winding Way, 14

12"
Daisy Field, 19
Feather Wreath, 24
Floral Spray, 29
Granny Smith's, 15
Winding Way, 14

12½"
Evening Flower, 39

13"
Celebration, 17
Lilac Leaf, 13
Rondo, 23

13½"
Floral Spray, 29

14"
Leaf & Tendril, 45

15"
Washington's Wreath, 40

17"
Evening Flower, 38

Rectangles
If you don't find the dimensions you need, match the height of your rectangle with border motifs and see if repeats fit into your rectangle area.

6" x 2"
Snow Blossom, 32

6" x 3"
Stardust, 68

7" x 3"
Heart's Flower, 34

7½" x 2½"
Yukon Cable, 49

9" x 2½"
Lilac Leaf, 13

9½" x 4"
Sea Serpent, 73

10" x 2½"
Yukon Cable, 49

10" x 3"
Winding Way, 14

10" x 6"
Best Foot Forward, 60

11½" x 3½"
Heart's Flower, 34

12½" x 2½"
Yukon Cable, 49

15" x 4½"
Evening Trumpet, 10
Floral Spray, 29

Triangles
(measured on short side)

3"
Lilting Leaf, 33

4½"
Berry Blossom, 25
Butterfly Dance, 58
Lilting Leaf, 33

5"
Celestial, 12
Fortune Flower, 27
He-Loves-Me, 55

5½"
Autumn Leaves, 26

6"
Cabbage Rose, 30
Desert Sunset, 65
Evening Flower, 39
Evening Trumpet, 11
Graceful Vine, 25
Grapevine, 41
Harvest Bloom, 52
Leaf & Tendril, 45

6½"
Bamboo, 21
Tulip Wreath, 57

7"
Daisy Field, 18
Summer Bloom, 43

7½"
Dragonfly, 21
Man in the Moon, 64
Rain or Shine, 65

8½"
Feather Wreath, 24
Sheriff's Badge, 86

9"
Bamboo, 21
Rainbow Sherbet, 64

9½"
Sheriff's Badge, 86

12"
Feather Wreath, 24

Octagons

5"
Springtime, 22

5½"
Snow Blossom, 32

6"
Leaf Spray, 37

7"
Celtic Chain, 16
Jaunty Jump-Ups, 48

7½"
Happy Days, 56

8"
Herbal Medley, 42

8½"
Crown, 86
Hearts & Flowers, 53

10"
Dolphin Bay, 75
Fortune Flower, 27

Borders
A motif that fits in a square can also be used for a border. Select one with the same measurement as the border width you wish to fill and repeat the design along the lengths.

2"
He-Loves-Me, 55
Jaunty Jump-Ups, 48
Leaf Spray, 37
Snow Blossom, 32
Teddy Bear, 84

Circle & Angle Templates

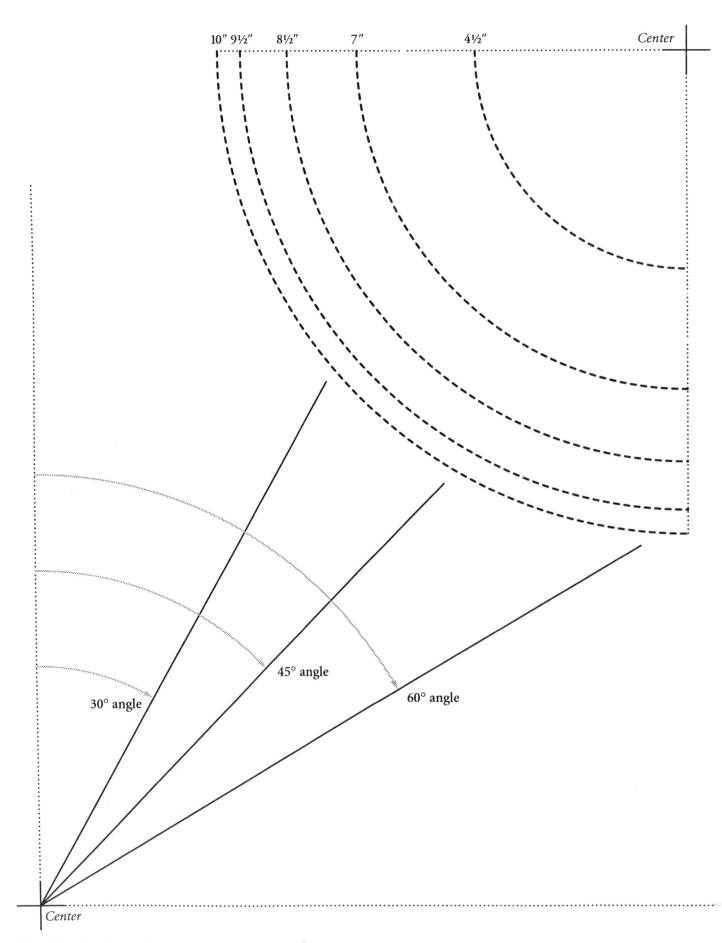

10" 9½" 8½" 7" 4½" Center

30° angle

45° angle

60° angle

Center